What Makes a Good City?

What Makes a Good City?

PUBLIC THEOLOGY AND THE URBAN CHURCH

Elaine Graham and Stephen Lowe

DARTON · LONGMAN + TODD

First published in 2009 by
Darton, Longman and Todd Ltd
1 Spencer Court
140–142 Wandsworth High Street
London SW18 4JJ

ISBN 978-0-232-52748-3

A catalogue record for this book is available from the British Library.

Phototypeset by Kerrypress Ltd, Luton, Bedfordshire
Printed and bound in Great Britain by Athenaeum Press, Gateshead, Tyne & Wear

To the men and women, lay and ordained, who keep the urban church alive

Contents

Foreword

by the Archbishop of York, Dr John Sentamu

The Church of England's parish system is far from perfect. Without it – as this book rightly states – many of our inner cities, outer estates and rural communities, 'would long ago have been abandoned to be replaced by gathered, suburban churches serving the comfortable with a comfortable gospel'.

I hope and pray that day never comes.

Elaine Graham and Stephen Lowe have produced a fine piece of work on what makes a good city and the role churches can play. I hope it will equip our churches with the knowledge to fulfil that role and stir them into action.

As a priest who has served in predominantly urban dioceses – Southwark, London and Birmingham – I saw all that was excellent and not so good about how inner-city churches fulfilled their calling. This book is a reality check that pulls no punches and leaves no stone unturned in assessing how we make church work in the urban context. It reaffirms to me that doing nothing is not an option.

I was reminded of what the great Archbishop of San Salvador, Oscar Romero, said in a sermon just minutes before his assassination: 'We know that every effort to improve society, above all when society is so full of injustice and sin, is an effort that God blesses; that God wants; that God demands of us.'

Our churches can be the place where the dreams and aspirations of a community find their fulfillment in a Christ-shaped reality. This book gives me cause for great hope in what is possible.

Introduction
Public Theology and the Urban Church

Imagine an organisation with 16,500 local outlets in every community in the land, 10,000 full-time employees and capital assets, excluding its buildings, of over £5 billion. It has 44 regional centres, each managing a substantial asset and property base – and all with some of the most significant buildings in their region – a footfall each week of one million worshippers and two million visitors every month, plus millions more using the buildings owned by the organisation and benefiting from the work sponsored by them. It is a major provider of education and the largest single provider of youth work in the country. This organisation, the Church of England, claims every citizen of this country as a parishioner, giving them rights in relation to their parish church and imposing responsibilities on the local church and its members to be, in the words of William Temple, 'an organisation which exists for the benefit of those who are not its members'.[1] Despite calls for disestablishment and the separation of religion and public life, many would acknowledge that without the Church of England, community cohesion in this country would not only be damaged but seriously fractured. Its clergy are often the last remaining professionals living in some of our neediest communities, and its buildings, in both rural and urban communities, are important symbols of continuity and service. The Church of England, despite secularist claims of its demise, remains the largest voluntary organisation in the country.

Christians are called to worship God. But they are also called through their study of Scripture and tradition to offer an incarnational presence for the world – the Word made flesh in the life and teaching of Jesus. So part of the task of the church is to be transformative, embodying vision and signalling justice. This is much more than service provision. It is about hope, transfiguration and the Kingdom. It is not just a 'mission statement', but is proclaimed in word and deed and is fuelled by values. It is a faith that is lived, practised and proclaimed day in day out. It arises out of what

Christians are called to do and be in community. This is a performative, practical theology, which is not just preaching *to* the world but incarnated *in* it. But what does it actually look like at the grass roots?

The Byker estate in Newcastle-upon-Tyne has had its problems since its construction in the 1930s. St Martin's was built as a parish hall in 1933 as a meeting place for the local community with chairs put out on Saturday evenings for worship on Sunday. In the 1970s it became a parish in its own right but by the 1990s its future was uncertain. The estate was becoming depopulated and the indices of multiple deprivation were among the highest in the country. The church seemed to be in terminal decline with falling numbers and very few children and families. But the parish priest and the Church Council members had a vision for its renewal, and the new St Martin's Byker was born. It was to be a partnership – an equal partnership of people from the community, the church and other community and voluntary organisations – which shares a common understanding that Every Person Matters. The new St Martin's centre now aims to meet the needs of everyone in a friendly, supportive and inclusive way that offers among other things a place to grow, a place to learn, a place to worship, a place to be heard, a safe and comfortable place that welcomes and cares, a future-orientated environment that enables people of all ages to develop to their fullest potential and a centre where people from the neighbourhood take an active part in decisions about the high-quality activities. There is a stream of incarnational practical theology running through the philosophy of St Martin's.

In July 2006 the new St Martin's was opened. It is an impressive building on two floors, with a full-scale children's centre run in partnership with Barnardo's. Over 1500 people a month come through the building, from childminders to toddlers, tea club members to cheerleaders, ballet dancers to brownies. The building is glazed so the outsider can see in and see the life and activity going on inside as well the warm and welcoming environment. There are no fences in this difficult area. How different from the barbed wire and locked doors of many of our church buildings.

Halifax Parish Church would not normally be considered as the natural setting for a major conference looking at the future of Halifax and Calderdale. A former textile town, perhaps now more famous as the home of HBOS (and its precursor the Halifax Building Society), it now has a substantial Muslim population and a passionate Black Chief Executive in Owen Williams. Its new Vicar, Hilary Barber, felt that religious groups had a contribution to make. 'The faith communities are already contributing a huge amount to society in Calderdale and the big issue is that they want to be taken seriously by both central and local Government, in terms of partnership and identifying a common vision for the future.' More than 150 people gathered in the medieval building for a whole day, eating and debating. They were from the local authority, the health authority, schools, voluntary organisations and the local MP. The faith leaders and members were sharing their visions and hopes with the ancient parish church fulfilling its traditional role as a major meeting place for the whole community. It's fair to say that only the Church of England could have called together such an event by providing such a neutral venue. Hilary Barber concluded at the end of the event: 'The challenge for the Council is to demonstrate that it is listening to the people of Calderdale and that it is going to show actively in the next 18 months how it is going to enable the faith communities to really engage with making Calderdale a happy place for everyone to live in.' Once again, vision and a demand for happiness in the communities in which we live is at the heart of the stated Christian ambition.

Gosport certainly does not have the vitality and reputation of its close neighbour, Portsmouth. At the end of a peninsular opposite Portsmouth Harbour, it is served by a desperately overcrowded A32 and is a southern community largely created for the Royal Navy whose needs have changed. There are enormous social housing estates in desperate need of modernisation or demolition. Yet within its boundaries there is substantial wealth at Lee-on-the-Solent and plans for substantial new housing development. The Diocese of Portsmouth and the Gosport deanery decided that it would be good to sponsor an event on what will make a good Gosport. The Chief Executive, Council officers, a local MP, health workers, local police in abundance, the churches and many voluntary sector organisations came together for a day, and, most importantly, made new relationships. Those serving local communities rarely have opportunities to meet with other agencies working in the same community with the same people. The days of social and community workers' lunches designed at least to get some of the professionals meeting together seemed to have disappeared in the world of performance targets. It seems that 'if it can't be measured then it shouldn't happen' is a new doctrine dominating local service delivery. Once again, it was the local church offering the opportunity for a community to stand back and reflect on where it is going, to offer vision, hope and transformation. Those who went away from the community centre that day were buzzing with excitement.

It was a similar energy that encouraged the Liverpool deanery of Wigan to challenge the local authority to become involved in a debate about the future of Wigan. The Policy Exchange think-tank recently identified Wigan as one of those northern towns whose citizens might do better if they migrated to Cambridge or some other booming south-eastern hub. In fact Wigan borough has a population of over 305,000 and is a 4-star performing local authority. It has a Premiership football team and an outstanding rugby league side, both playing at the new JJB stadium. Wigan Council, aware that government policy was moving away from a focus on regeneration and on to an agenda of worklessness, invited the churches to share in a cross-sector day entitled 'What Makes Wigan Work'. There are 190,800 people in Wigan of working age, of whom 34,500 are workless. The largest group of claimants are those on incapacity benefit, many of whom are suffering from stress-related illnesses. The JJB stadium was home to the day conference that had participants grouped around tables in interdisciplinary working groups. The members were all made to work with the conference, producing a published report that is full of aspiration and commitment to a better way of working together as agencies con-cerned with the well-being of Wigan and its citizens. Of course there was much to complain about. The voluntary and community sector felt victimised by short-term funding and a lack of real participation in decision-making. The churches felt their potential and contribution had often been forgotten. There was unanimity about the success of the day and a commitment from the Chief Executive to call back the conference in a year's time to report on progress and achievements. The stimulus for the day had come from the churches and the day focused, despite the motives behind the Government's agenda, on improving well-being and happiness for the citizens of Wigan.

These are all examples of ways in which the church has taken the lead in encouraging local people to think about their neighbourhoods. In Byker it has involved local people taking an initiative to change the nature of the church's mission and presence within that community. It involved them in developing a vision for the future of their work and translating that vision into a new physical presence, which has undoubtedly changed people's lives and made Byker a much more attractive place for people to live. In Halifax, Gosport and Wigan the church has sat down with hundreds of others – professionals, voluntary groups and residents – and asked questions about what makes a good city/community and what would improve the happiness and well-being of the people whom it serves. The distinctive contributions of faith have acted as a catalyst to others to articulate what values are significant for *any* definition of a 'good city'. But these are also graphic illustrations of how the church's physical presence in a neighbourhood as a bearer of memory, sanctifying space and place, has enabled others to engage with questions of meaning and vision.

The distinctive marks of urban church in these contexts might be described as follows:

- uniquely local, with a long-term presence and commitment to that space and place;
- offering care and service to the community;
- embodying a vision of hope, forgiveness and transcendence.

Government and the faith communities: why don't they get it?

There is a very real problem at national and local levels over the relationship between the faith communities and government. Local government has struggled to discover what might be termed a basic 'religious literacy' – that is, a competent level of knowledge and empathy about the nature of religious faith and its effects on believers – among both its members and officers. As a result, Christian groups in particular have suffered irrational prejudice against their funding applications and a lack of understanding of the nature and sometimes fragility of the local church. There is a perception, perhaps justified, that it has been easier for Islamic groups to receive financial support than other faith groups. There have been numerous examples of local authorities inviting consultation with local faith groups and failing to invite any Christians!

There seem to be two reasons for these problems. As secularisation makes further inroads into British society, it becomes less likely that many members of society will have first-hand experience of belonging to a major faith tradition. Whether or not the precepts of what may be termed the 'new secularism' (see Chapter 5) take real root in British hearts and minds, the trends suggest that over the next generation we will move from a sociology of a nominally religious and 'lapsed' population to a situation of an increasing bifurcation between a religiously committed minority (of many faiths) and a religiously unaffiliated majority. This means that many public servants, particularly in local government, have little working knowledge of religion, with resulting lack of 'religious literacy' when it comes to dealing with matters of religion in relation to law, child protection, health care, death and bereavement and the role of faith in the community.

The picture is not entirely bleak. The emergency services, and in particular the police, recognised the problem several years ago, and organisations like St Philip's Centre in Leicester, Bradford Churches for Dialogue and Diversity, Faith Literacy UK in London and the Yorkshire and Humberside Regional Churches Commission, have been offering training. The sophistication of the relationships that most police forces have with their local faith communities is a tribute to both the training and the investment of energy and commitment on their part.

After years of debate, admittedly made more difficult by the faith communities themselves, it looks as if a national programme of religious literacy training will be offered with financial support from the Department of Communities and Local Government. What is now vital is a commitment from the Local Government Association and ministers to ensure that the training developed becomes a requirement for officers and members working in a multi-faith, multi-cultural context.

Secondly, there can be little doubt that the terrorism agenda has seriously unbalanced government relationships with the faith communities. At one stage primary responsibility for part of this relationship rested with the Home Office but in more recent years this has passed to Communities and Local Government with a particular emphasis on religious extremism. Some government policy has been ill-informed. A grant was given to establish regional faith forums when many already existed. The Faith Communities Capacity Building Programme initially gave grants for a year when the Government itself was acknowledging that grants for less than three years did more harm than good. At local level, faith leaders' meetings have been taking place for many years often chaired by the diocesan bishop. These have proved significant meeting places for the faith communities where Jews, Muslims, Sikhs, Hindus, Christians and Buddhists have been able to meet regularly as respected friends with a common concern for avoiding conflict and increasing local partnership. Funding and support for these vital parts of the faith fabric of this nation has not been forthcoming, yet they are increasingly used by local authorities and statutory agencies as points of contact with the faith communities.

Even more complex has been the Labour Government's relationship with the Church of England. Part of the problem is the perpetual struggle within prime ministers and ministers over their own personal religious beliefs, or lack of them, and the national dialogue over secularism and atheism that has grown more stormy since 9/11 and 7/7. Since Alistair Campbell's famous statement that 'We don't do God', the church has worked with two prime ministers whose faith is clearly of great importance to them. Fortunately we are not possessed with the paradox of the United States' political system, which separates church and state, where the strength of the religious Right makes it impossible for anyone but a practising Christian to aspire to the presidency. Yet there is still a great degree of inconsistency in the way individual ministers deal with religious groups, in a way that suggests sheer ignorance rather than prejudice. For example, when the Secretary of State for Communities and Local Government, Hazel Blears, responding to the launch of *Moral But No Compass* in May 2008, stated on the BBC Radio 4 *Sunday* programme, that 'we live in a secular democracy', she was not only factually incorrect but demonstrated an extraordinary misreading of British constitutional history, not least in her complete oversight of the existence of the established churches in England and Scotland! The complaint that government simply did not know or understand the extent of the Church of England's contribution to the social welfare fabric of this country was subsequently denied, yet, as we will argue in Chapter 8, evidentially correct. Off the record, civil servants will acknowledge that all is not well, yet ministers are left to pronounce from a position of ignorance at best, or prejudice at worst.

Part of the problem rests in the church's own complicated structures. There is a tendency to see the Church of England as a hierarchical system with the Archbishop of Canterbury as some sort of papal supreme and the Archbishop of York as his northern deputy. If they find difficulty with anything the church has said and done in all its manifestations then a phone call to the Archbishop is seen as the way to sort it out. The Church of England is a many-headed complex organisation with most authority lying at diocesan level with the diocesan bishops. There is no possibility of archbishops wielding hierarchical power, but every possibility of them exercising enormous influence from the respect they have gained from colleagues. Certainly this is the case with the present incumbents. The chance of the Archbishop of Canterbury being able to influence what is happening in the minister's constituency is like asking the President of FIFA to influence team selection at Crewe Alexandra.

Admittedly, conversations do take place between archbishops, bishops, members of the Archbishops' Council staff and government ministers. The church itself is not very good at communicating to other interested parties some of the outcomes of these meetings, sometimes creating the impression of an organisation guarding its own internal sectional interests. Bishops in the Lords have their own platform, sometimes very individual and not necessarily reflecting an accepted church policy. No wonder then that it is difficult for ministers to know exactly what they are dealing with; and yet those who have addressed the General Synod have seen this as a significant political event. After all, as the report *Moral But No Compass* revealed, the Church of England is the largest voluntary organisation in the country, and a large majority of voters still claim membership of churches, chapels, synagogues, temples and mosques! While we do not advocate simply reducing the Church of England or any faith-based organisation to the status of simply another part of the voluntary sector, this is a glaring example of the way in which faith and government alike must take the citizenship role of religious believers seriously.

The Archbishop of Canterbury, Rowan Williams, provoked political hysteria in February 2008 when he suggested that some concessions might be offered under English law to alternative systems, such as Sharia, in order to acknowledge the religious and cultural sensibilities of British Muslims and other minorities (Higton, 2008; Chaplin, 2008). Now that the debate has cooled somewhat it is clear that the Archbishop was speaking into a highly febrile atmosphere, in which the public role of religion is increasingly regarded with suspicion. There is little patience on the part of government or media to give measured consideration to the complexities of how a nation might balance respect for religious diversity, and a mature acknowledgement of the influence of religion on the lives of millions of its members, with concern for freedom of speech and the principles of liberal democracy. The way in which Rowan Williams was shouted down for even raising these issues is a discouraging reflection of our lack of political sophistication in this respect.

This is the context in which the urban church is working: not simply providing services or facilities for its own membership or speaking a private language, but engaged in *public* theology. It needs to face the challenges of conducting strategic partnerships; of engaging with anxieties about religion as an extremist, proselytising divisive social influence (which nevertheless have to be acknowledged as legitimate); and of providing a coherent, theologically rooted account of why it is doing all this. What, therefore, does a public theology that addresses the challenges of urban life and faith need to look like?

What's the use of theology?

The examples at the beginning of this chapter – like so many of the experiences on which we will be drawing for this book – inherit a rich tradition of Establishment, which has arguably served the urban Church of England well (cf. ACUPA, 1985) but increasingly is in need of re-examination in the light of the following trends:

- calls for disestablishment
- the challenges of 'new secularism'
- a turn to more 'ecclesial' and confessional theological perspectives.

In many respects, despite their clear virtues, the kind of work being carried out in Newcastle, Wigan, Halifax and Gosport requires constant theological reinvigoration. We will therefore argue for a renewed 'public theology' that stands in a largely liberal revisionist tradition but which is also mindful that it no longer speaks into any kind of consensus, either within the churches or beyond, of what the future priorities should be. We will argue that such a theological stance can be justified against both secularist and neo-orthodox critics, but that changing times require its renewal.

In our discussion of how theology informs and guides the praxis of the urban church, we follow the argument of Graham, Walton and Ward (2005; 2007) in arguing that theology must be seen primarily as a practical discourse or 'practical wisdom' with the objective of shaping faithful individuals and communities. 'Talk about God' originates in the challenges of everyday living, and seeks to articulate the values and norms by which Christians can chart their journeys of faith. According to Graham, Walton and Ward, there are three main dimensions to which such a practical theology must address itself: induction and nurture of individuals, the corporate identity and ethos of the Body of Christ, and the relationship between the claims of the Gospel and the wider culture beyond the church – be that of dialogue, outreach or proclamation (Graham, Walton and Ward, 2005: 10–11).

In extending that work into public theology, our interest is in addressing the following practical questions:

- What does it mean for all baptised Christians to exercise their vocation in the changing contexts of a globalised, urbanising world, and how can they be nurtured and supported in that witness – in personal prayer and study, corporate worship and theological education? How do the 'base elements' of Christian theology – Scripture, tradition, reason and experience – combine into the unique genetic code that instructs and gives life to the urban church (Graham, Walton and Ward, 2007: 2)?

- What shape should the urban church assume, as local, national and global fellowships of faith? Does the parish system, which is deeply ingrained into the DNA of the Church of England, have any further relevance or utility today? What does the incarnated presence of the local church say, theologically, about the reality and activity of God in that place?

- What understanding of the nature of ministry and God's mission to the world should underpin the shape and priorities of the urban church?

- What is distinctive about the urban church's contribution to the life of the wider community? Is it legitimate to admit the contribution of faith-based organisations and theologically informed debate into the public domain when signs are that Britain is increasingly becoming 'post-Christian'?

We will argue that, essentially, the theological task for the urban church is not about introducing God or a particular pattern of spirituality or belief into the city, but about discerning the drama of creation, incarnation and redemption as it unfolds in the 'everyday' faithfulness of the city.

About the book

This book is the result of collaboration between an urban practitioner with a lifetime of experience in urban ministry and an academic theologian who stresses the primacy of context and experience for theological understanding. Over nearly ten years, we have met together frequently, initially as work consultants for one another, and then, between 2004 and 2006, as fellow members of the Commission for Urban Life and Faith. It is out of that work, and our reflections on Stephen's role as Bishop for Urban Life and Faith for the Church of England, that this book has emerged. We hope it will be of interest to urban ministers, students, policy-makers and politicians: all those who have the good of our cities at heart, and all those who work for greater understanding, justice and equity in church and society.

In Chapter 1, we consider the broad metaphors by which the direction of the urban church might be regulated, and how the twin imperatives of 'discipleship' and 'citizenship' might function to express the tension, but ultimately the synthesis, between engagement and prophecy in the name of a Gospel that both affirms and transforms human affairs. Using Augustine's *City of God*, a classic of Christian theology, this chapter will shape the contours of an urban, public theology that is capable both of nurturing the faithful, distinctive practice of the local church and of informing an engaged and 'incarnational' presence in public affairs.

Chapter 2 will engage in a critique of recent official reports on urban life and faith, including the Commission for Urban Life and Faith's report, *Faithful Cities: A Call for Celebration, Vision and Justice* (2006). Its major conclusions regarding the enduring significance of faith-based contributions to local neighbourhoods, in the shape of 'faithful capital', its analysis of government policy on urban regeneration and its attempt to exercise a particular theological method will all be examined. Its core criteria around the question, 'What makes a good city?' will be compared with other perspectives on the 'harmonious' and 'human' city. The chapter will evaluate how successfully *Faithful Cities* reflected contemporary trends in social policy and urban theory and what its impact tells us about church–state relations and the significance of public theology for the urban church.

Chapter 3 develops a further major theme of the book, emphasising how the so-called 'spatial turn' in both urban theory and theology offers rich potential for an understanding of the nature of the urban church in plural society. The significance of a trinitarian theology in which 'God takes place', a commitment to localism and the sacredness of space and place, all emerge as central and enduring themes for the practice of the urban church.

Chapter 4 considers the continuing polarisation between rich and poor, and argues that the social exclusion of many of our most marginalised urban communities remains one of the most significant challenges. Despite their achievements in revitalising the local economy of many English cities, regeneration policies have done little to narrow the gulf of wealth, opportunity or educational aspiration. This chapter argues that theological traditions of God's 'preferential option for the poor' and an open, inclusive hospitality are the well-springs of the local church's presence and engagement.

Faithful Cities began to address the impact of globalisation on urban life and faith, and to suggest ways in which the local church might relate to an increasingly plural culture. In Chapter 5, we review current debates about the future of multi-culturalism in the UK and consider whether government concerns for social cohesion have adequately addressed the needs of different communities. The chapter will explore how resources from biblical literature might inform theological and practical responses to questions of diversity and difference.

Chapter 6 will consider some of the thinking behind strategies for urban regeneration that use the so-called 'cultural industries' as the catalyst for economic revival. Liverpool's year of culture 2008 has been an outstanding success, but there are questions to be asked about whose 'culture' this is, and how 'religion' is or is not being incorporated into the aspirations of cultural renaissance. We will argue that the urban church's stress on valuing localism, its work in nurturing the language of narrative, memory and value, and its striving to nurture sacred space in the midst of the everyday are all invaluable aspects of its contribution to the 'good city'.

The 'good city' depends on fostering active citizenship, but very often urban communities suffer from a democratic deficit – and the church seldom models anything much better. *Faithful Cities* called for greater empowerment of urban communities, but gave few clues as to how this might happen. Chapter 7 examines one strategy of empowerment, broad-based organising, and argues that its emphasis on building relationships of trust and mutuality finds deep resonance in theological themes of unconditional love and justice. It offers a manifesto for equipping the urban church with a strategy for change that powerfully links the personal and the political.

Chapter 8 begins to draw together conclusions concerning the future viability of the urban church. Increasingly, the local urban church will be a microcosm of a global community, as congregations reflect the patterns of migration from the global South. Wider political trends will also present opportunities and challenges to the urban church, as government and tradition alike express interest in mobilising faith groups in the delivery of welfare. Despite its resilience, the urban church is confronted by major demographic and financial crises which will require radical restructuring: can it survive, and in what shape?

1
Citizens or Disciples?

Introduction

Christianity has been an urban religion since its very beginnings, and
sociological and geopolitical factors associated with its urban origins
undoubtedly contributed to its rapid missionary spread throughout the
Roman Empire (Gillett, 2005: 25–6). The experience of urban civilisation
also infuses biblical imagery, such as that of the 'new Jerusalem' of
Revelation. Even the development of Christian doctrine has been shaped
by the opportunities and challenges of urban living as it has been presented
to every generation. If, as we suggested in the Introduction, the history of
Christian theology was to be written contextually, as a body of practical
wisdom, then the tasks of urban life and faith become the foundations
upon which the staple values of the Gospel are laid bare: how one lives
with the tension between conducting oneself as a citizen of the earthly and
of the heavenly city; how the *ekklesia*, or household of God, is to be
governed amidst a plurality of households; and what kind of public
significance might follow from a profession of belief and trust in the risen
Jesus Christ. Cities have perennially been hubs of civilisation and centres of
trade and exchange, of the exercise of imperial power and military strategy
and the cultivation of the arts; but also have inevitably been the places in
which Christians of every generation have been called to reflect on and to
exercise their vocation. In other words, they have been the places where
'Christ' and 'culture' meet.

While it is not our intention in this chapter to write a systematic history
of a discipline called 'urban theology', we do wish to indicate some ways in

which successive generations have approached the practical 'delights, injustices and needs' of urban living. For these have been the contexts out of which have been crafted new understandings of the nature of God, the world and human flourishing, which in turn have contributed to the inherited wisdom of theological tradition.

In particular, we want to begin to consider two different models for theology to inform the life and witness of the urban church and of the ways in which the sources of the Christian tradition might inform contemporary practice. There are choices to be made. Does the Gospel call Christians to seek what is often termed 'the common good' and to immerse themselves in wider society, to collaborate with those of other faiths and none in the name of a shared humanity? Or is the Christian calling a matter of building up the distinctive identity of the church as a counter-cultural reality that is not answerable to the precepts of secular reason? We might characterise these as two contrasting understandings of the prospect of how theology 'goes public':

1   Active engagement with a pluralist culture and liberal state in the name of identifying universal human principles, moral values – such as in a shared language of the common good. What we might term a 'public' urban theology.

2   Insistence on a more exclusivist stance in order to protect integrity of gospel values in a pluralist world. It is assumed that the trappings of Western modernity, for example pluralism, civil religion and liberalism (including theology that seeks to 'correlate' with non-Christian values), are inimical to true and radical discipleship. What we might term an 'ecclesial' urban theology.

This tension is well encapsulated in this quotation from the American theologian Kristin Heyer:

One of the issues brought to the fore in the process is how theologies 'go public' – whether, for example, the inevitability of the particular origin and context of religious symbols and beliefs renders them decipherable and meaningful only within the community of 'origin', or whether such particularity *may actually enable* more broadly compelling meaning or a public voice for theology ... [T]hese different approaches call into question whether 'taking theology public' constitutes an imperative for theology or instead poses dangers to the theological enterprise. (Heyer, 2004: 308)

We are going to characterise these two perspectives as stressing, respectively, the virtues of 'citizenship' versus 'discipleship'. While in reality they are not mutually exclusive, they serve as ideal types that have consistently informed Christian theological debate. When the letter to the Romans exhorts its listeners to 'be not conformed but transformed' to the world, the writer is reflecting the debate that Christians have always had concerning whether baptism and the believer's new life in Christ requires a withdrawal and separation from the conventions of this world, or whether the proper calling of faith is to work for the redemption of the world as the place in which God as creator, as incarnate Son and animating Spirit is eternally active. The twentieth-century theologian H. Richard Niebuhr characterises this perennial tension as one between the poles of 'Christ' and 'culture' (H. R. Niebuhr, 1951); but essentially, it is an issue about whether the revelation of God takes place primarily through the traditions and practices of the church, or whether the 'secular' realms of nature, culture, science and politics can also point us towards the truth.

In terms of the relevance of such theologies of 'revelation' and 'reason' and the sensibilities of 'discipleship' and 'citizenship' for the urban church, therefore, we are concerned to articulate the essential task of theology for our work, both in directing the lives of the faithful, but also in adjudicating how theological principles might 'speak' into the public domain. The Anglican social tradition out of which we both write – and the Church of England in which Stephen has served – has leaned towards a more 'public' theology by virtue of its Established nature, affirming an essential convergence between Christian values and those of wider culture. In an increasingly secular, pluralist context, however, this may not necessarily be the case; and it may be time for the urban church to eschew the idea of 'baptising' the surrounding culture in favour of a practical theology that emphasises a more distinctive, counter-cultural, even prophetic ethic.

We will trace a movement through the twentieth and twenty-first centuries, therefore, away from 'liberal' or public theologies which worked dialogically with secular theories and trends – 'letting the world set the agenda' – to 'post-liberal' or ecclesial theologies, which stress the particularity of Christian identity grounded in the distinctiveness of doctrine or tradition and embodied in the worshipping/sacramental life of the church.

Our conclusion will be that the twin poles of public and ecclesial need to be held in tension; that although theology is revealed in divine teaching, it must be tested 'in public'. Nevertheless, the church is ultimately a public undertaking, which necessarily proclaims a theology of 'God-in-the-world, *to* the world' (Graham, 2004: 399), and thus can never restrict its conversation, nor its partnerships, to those of an ecclesial nature alone.

In the process, we will also draw on the writing of one major theologian, who was very concerned about the nature of Christian civic responsibility in the context of ancient Rome: that is the theologian Augustine of Hippo, a North African monk and civil servant of the fifth century CE. His treatise *City of God* was all about where urban Christians should place their ultimate loyalty: to the state, to earthly rulers, or to the world to come, the Kingdom of God? Part of the intention of this chapter is, therefore, to put contemporary concerns into conversation with a classic of Christian theology, and to indicate that the twin callings of the public and the ecclesial, to be citizen or disciple, have always been at the heart of theological debate.

The nature of public theology

This section will examine the tradition of 'public theology', consider its critics, and advance a revised model of theological reflection on urban life and faith that is capable of nurturing citisenship and discipleship in a creative fashion. We began to map out the contours of 'public theology' in the Introduction; definitions and traditions vary, but the following list describes some of its key manifestations.

First, there is the type of public theology that engages with issues of public policy from a faith-based perspective. This might be in the pro-nouncements of theologians, church reports or church leaders, but is 'an attempt to make the moral implications of the Christian faith available to the larger society in a publicly intelligible manner' (Breitenberg, 2003: 64). Reports such as *Faith in the City* (ACUPA, 1985) and *Faithful Cities* (CULF, 2006), which will form the basis of Chapter 2, would be examples of church-sponsored commentary on a particular issue of public policy, namely the state of our cities and towns. Public theology embraces more than just political theology, so it is concerned not only with the affairs of state, but those of a variety of 'publics', such as business and the market, science and philosophy, family life, racial justice, voluntary organisations and popular culture, including the news media, entertainment and the arts: any institution that shapes the way we think, relate or live in the world. The statements of a bishop or archbishop on the credit crunch, global poverty or international affairs also represent a form of theology 'going public', since they are concerned with the relevance of faith for the wider social and cultural context beyond the institutional churches.

A second dimension might be concerned with the processes of guidance or formation that equip Christians (ordained and lay) to exercise faithful witness in relation to the secular world, especially perhaps the world of work. This is about a 'public' theology that helps people become more articulate and confident in relating the premises of faith to the challenges of contemporary living, both as individual Christians and the corporate body of Christ, and how church life can help its members to relate with integrity to public institutions such as the media, public services, education or industry. For many lay people, especially those in secular occupations, however, the challenge of contemporary life is twofold: just as public life is becoming increasingly functionally secular or religiously 'illiterate', so many local churches are becoming 'privatised' and more concerned with personal spirituality or the maintenance of their own structures and activities. There is a pressing need for a public theology that confers confidence and the opportunity to 'reflect theologically' on daily life.

A third dimension could be a study of how a faith-commitment might form the public conduct of politicians, and how they choose to mediate that into the public square (de Gruchy, 2007; Gay, 2007; Graham, 2009c). This is partly a case study in how the 'private' convictions of an individual translate into a public, institutional setting of political debate and policy. But as Alastair Campbell's famous warning to an interviewer wishing to interrogate Tony Blair on his religious beliefs – 'We don't do God' – signals, there is considerable resistance to politicians' going public, as well as increasing public skepticism in the face of religious extremism (Graham, 2009a). While this is not our primary concern, we will return in Chapter 5 to the broader question of how far religious reasoning is an acceptable form of public discourse or whether it must be 'bracketed out' of secular democratic debate.

The roots of public theology

Although Christians have always been exercised by questions of how to conduct themselves in relation to public or non-ecclesial institutions, as well as to non-believers, the term 'public theology' is surprisingly recent. The term was only coined by the American scholar Martin Marty in 1974. Marty wanted to delineate a tradition in theological thought that offered some clarity about the public bearing of Christian faith, and in particular the characteristics of churches' and individuals' engagement in public and social issues. In Western societies, we tend to take for granted the notion of religious belief as a matter of personal choice, but Marty is reminding us that religion is also 'public' in that faith always assumes an institutional and collective expression, and religious teachings also shape our culture in terms of moral teaching and social activism.

Marty identifies two strands of what he calls 'public theology' within American life, with roots in late nineteenth- and twentieth-century church and society. First, he focuses on the writing and activism of church leaders concerned to relate their experiences of ministry into strategies for social change. He nominates Walter Rauschenbusch (1861–1918), a Baptist minister and advocate of the 'Social Gospel', as an exemplary figure in this respect. Against a prevailing orthodoxy within American Protestantism towards individualism and individual salvation, Rauschenbusch adopted an alternative perspective, shaped by his ministry in the notorious 'Hell's Kitchen' neighbourhood of New York at the end of the nineteenth century. This was a society rapidly industrialising, but with massive poverty and poor conditions for the workers. In the face of a theology that assumed social structures and social conditions were ordained by God, Rauschenbusch preached about the immanence of the Kingdom of God, and an interpretation of the ministry of Jesus that stressed his identification with human suffering and the ethical and political significance of the Gospel (Gillett, 2005: 22–3).

Rauschenbusch embraced a form of Christian socialism, calling for fundamental changes to society and economy, and the abolition of capitalism. He saw this as the tangible and temporal means of achieving the Kingdom of God; it was the task of the church and all Christians to effect this programme of social transformation in the name of the Gospel. The central role of the church is to usher in this new social order, to be the bearer of that message of hope, not least in the way it embodies characteristics of compassion for the poor, reconciliation of social divisions between different classes, ethnic groups and so on. Just as God reaches out to humanity in the person of Jesus, Rauschenbusch argued, so too now must the church be a channel of God's love in the world.

But Marty also claims that leading politicians of the American Revolution, such as Benjamin Franklin and Abraham Lincoln, were also practitioners of 'public theology', since they used religious or theological resources 'in order to make sense of the American experience' (Marty, 1974: 333). They drew on a deep repository of religious motifs both to inform their own political strategies and to call forth reflection on the destiny of America as a nation. These two traditions, of activism for social change and public comment from a theological perspective, fuse, says Marty, in the person of Reinhold Niebuhr (1892–1971), the liberal Protestant academic, in that he was both an interpreter of American religious social behaviour – the activities of the churches and church people in public life – and a major contributor to debate about public issues from a theological perspective. He was convinced of the essentially practical and ethical nature of theology in informing and guiding concrete values and situations. Niebuhr's argument was that Christianity is more than simply about personal salvation or 'spiritual' questions. It has a public bearing that goes further even than thinking about the 'public' impact of the church as institution. He held a conviction that it is acceptable, even essential, for Christians to engage in matters to do with the ordering of our common life, to be concerned with the ordering of human affairs beyond the ecclesial, to embrace the whole of society and to introduce a theological perspective into public debate. This is thus theology that addresses questions of public significance, seeks to influence a wider culture and helps to shape the way problems and policies are addressed (Marty, 1974: 334ff.; Atherton, 2000: 1–24).

Niebuhr has his critics, as Marty concedes. He did not have a very strong doctrine of the church, seeing his theology rather more in terms of practical wisdom and ethical discourse addressed to society at large, but which is vulnerable to the charge that it seems to exist independently of the corporate life, traditions and worship of any particular community of faith. Does this mean, however, that it is possible to have theology without and outwith the church? From what place, then, does theology speak, and where does it stand: is it the invention of public intellectuals, or does it need to be rooted and cultivated in the liturgical and biblical traditions of church practice? As we will see, these criticisms resurface in the work of a later generation of more ecclesially minded theologians. Despite being immensely well known and widely read in terms of his contributions to public policy and popular debate, and as an observer of religion and

'American values', this was only possible because Niebuhr was confident that his audience shared his frame of reference. Even if they were Jewish or agnostic, they did not question his assumption that his brand of liberal Protestantism could easily be equated with the core values of the American people.

There is also a strong European and British tradition of public theology. In a similar spirit to Marty, the Scottish theologian Duncan Forrester assembles a kind of 'family tree' of nineteenth- and twentieth-century proto-public theologians: Karl Barth, Dietrich Bonhoeffer, Reinhold Niebuhr, William Temple and Ronald Preston. William Temple (1881–1944) was an Establishment figure, a Christian socialist, who saw it as a natural extension of his role as bishop and archbishop in the Church of England to engage in dialogue with policy-makers and politicians, to speak out on social issues and to write about the theological principles that should inform society. This is a powerful model of what has come to be known as 'public' theology: 'At every level the church of Jesus Christ is faced with the challenge of William Temple, who said that the church is an organisation which exists for the sake of those who never darken its doors' (Forrester, 2001: 212). This reflects a high doctrine of creation, of God at work in human history and an assurance that the church seeks the fulfilment of the Kingdom in the well-being of the world. In Forrester's own words, public theology places the 'welfare of the city' over the 'interests of the Church' (Forrester, 2004: 6).

> Expressed in terms of the Christian tradition, public theology intends to provide theologically informed interpretations of and guidance for individuals, faith communities, and the institutions and interactions of civil society, in ways that are understandable, assessable, and possibly convincing to those inside the church and those outside as well. Public theologians thus seek to communicate, by means that are intelligible and assayable to all, how Christian beliefs and practices bear, both descriptively and prescriptively, on public life and the common good, and in so doing possibly persuade and move to action both Christians and non-Christians. (Breitenberg, 2003: 66)

This tradition of public theology is evident within some notable examples of writing on the urban church. In his book *Church and People in an Industrial* City, for example, which calls for new structures of parish life and industrial mission in order to meet the needs of major industrial cities, E. R. ('Ted') Wickham argues that mission is less about calling people out of the world into the church and more do with the church permeating all aspects of human life (Wickham, 1958: 227–8). The Gospel witnesses to the Person of Christ as 'the Word made Flesh, the supreme sanction and fulfilment of the truth; He is God revealed in history in the only way that man could understand Him, in whom the Kingdom is supremely established, who wills to incorporate all men into Himself making them instruments of His Kingdom, who will subdue all things and subject them to the Father' (Wickham, 1958: 234–5).

This theology of God at work in human affairs, of the Gospel calling Christians into the secular domain, continues through the mid twentieth century and arguably finds its apotheosis in Harvey Cox's *The Secular City* (1965). Rather than lamenting the trends within Western urbanisation that contributed to the decline of institutional religion throughout the nineteenth and twentieth centuries, Cox chooses to celebrate secularisation as evidenced within the modern industrial city. Cox welcomes what he sees as

> the loosing of the world from religious and quasi-religious understandings of itself, the dispelling of all closed world-views, the breaking of all supernatural myths and sacred symbols ... Secularization is man [sic] turning his attention away from worlds beyond and toward this world and this time ... It is what Dietrich Bonhoeffer in 1944 called 'man's coming of age'. (Cox, 1965: 2)

Cox spent a year in Berlin in the early 1960s, immersing himself in Bonhoeffer's work, and the latter's emphasis on a costly, kenotic discipleship that necessarily outgrows the securities of institutional religion in favour of a more humanistic religious quest is clear. But another influence is the sociological theory of modernity. The city is characterised as the place in which human autonomy and self-realisation might flourish, unhindered by tradition or conservatism. Freedom of speech and thought, pluralism and tolerance – all quintessential hallmarks of the modern industrial city – are the wellsprings of the secular way of life. Religion is gradually driven to the margins of public life, ceasing to be the overarching framework by which people order their lives. Yet this is a necessary part of the inevitable, irreversible and inexorable march of secularisation, for if religion stands for an infantile dependence of humanity on an authoritarian God, such 'bondage to the past' in the shape of superstition, irrationality, neurosis and dependence needs to be cast out like so many demons.

> Men must be called away from their fascination with other worlds –
> astrological, metaphysical, or religious – and summoned to confront
> the concrete issues of this one, 'wherein alone the call of God can be
> found'. They must be freed from the narcotic vagaries through which
> they wrongly perceive the social reality around them, and from
> habitual forms of action or inaction stemming from these illusions.
> This is the work of social exorcism. It was carried out by Jesus; his
> church should be expected to carry on this same work. (Cox, 1965:
> 154)

So religious activity must accommodate itself to the secular city; and the message of Christianity must express itself in terms comprehensible to secular humanity. The answer is to politicise the Gospel, to transform Christian practice into social transformation. Cox describes the church as 'God's Avant-garde' (1965: 128), and the boundaries of the institutional church dissolve into progressive social movements. It must jettison its own illusions of its own permanence and self-sufficiency in order to see itself not as an end in itself but as the instrument of God's purposes in the world. Its authority comes not from some 'supernatural' status or from its past glories, but from its credibility as a catalyst for change and empowerment, allowing itself 'to be broken and reshaped continuously by God's continuous action' (Cox, 1965: 105).

Central to these understandings of public theology is a correspondence between the religious and non-religious public. In the production of public theology the community of faith needs to find a language and an agenda which is meaningful to those both inside and outside the immediate community or tradition of faith, persuasive to both communities and finally contributing to the common good. So these are some of the contours of a public urban theology which seeks to share in the common life of the city, of fulfilling one's vocation as *citizen*, of contributing to a language of the common good, of assisting a debate about 'what makes a good city' from the perspective of shared values. This tradition is grounded in a strong affirmation of what John Calvin termed 'common grace': the notion that while there may be specific and unique revelation through the tradition – and for Christians, specifically in the person and work of Christ – God has also created other means by which others might be drawn to glimpse salvation: reason, secular knowledge and the striving of the human spirit for liberation.

Criticisms of public theology

Critics of public theology argue that theology cannot be derived from common reason or secular sources. Mindful of the question, 'From where does theology speak?' they argue that it is illegitimate to assume that theology can adopt the view from nowhere, and presumptive to conduct theological debate for the benefit of those outside the church. What matters is to cultivate the Christian virtues as embodied in its own tradition, to forge a distinctive community that is its own polis and not attempt any kind of correlation with public values. Public theology is too subservient to prevailing interests, such as the state or capitalism. It is the outworking of a declining and desperate institution that needs to be needed and so allows itself to be co-opted by the status quo. This silences the prophetic witness of the Gospel and reduces the church to a kind of instrumentalism. This is relevant when we come to think of debates about the 'rebranding' of church welfare services or churches required to enter the 'contract culture' (see Chapter 8).

A second criticism is that public theology spends too much time defining itself and not enough simply pursuing a decisive Christian witness in society. There is too much theory and not enough practice. It is insufficiently critical of its own sociology of knowledge. For all its talk of a multiplicity of publics, it remains in the ivory tower of academic speculation. Similarly, critics argue that public theology is too dependent on the specific contexts of its birth – liberal democracy in the USA and Establishment in the UK – to transcend these circumstances and address radically different societies or come to terms with the contradictions of liberalism and the collapse of Christendom. Its respect for 'secular reason' is not reciprocated: it is tolerated at best and increasingly marginal.

'Ecclesial' social ethics

If the mainstream tradition of 'public theology' rests upon an active engagement with pluralist culture and liberal state in the name of identifying common human morality and shared language of good, then an alternative tradition should also be considered. It places greater insistence on a more exclusivist stance in order to protect the integrity of gospel values in a hostile world. It is assumed that the trappings of Western modernity, such as pluralism, civil religion and liberalism (including theology that seeks to 'correlate' with non-Christian values) are inimical to true and radical discipleship. Thus, Christian theology cannot be 'public' in the sense of appealing to a foundational or universal human religious experience; rather, '[t]he primary task of theology … is Christian self-description, not correlation with universal human quests for ultimate meaning' (Sanks, 1993).

This kind of 'ecclesial' theology owes much to the philosophy of postmodernism, and especially the contention that we no longer live in a world of consensus, of grand narratives and universal truths. As a result, there is no such thing as 'common wisdom' to which all people of good faith – religious or not – can subscribe. This is also a reaction against the tendency of modern theology from the eighteenth century onwards, which understood the job of the theologian as demonstrating that modern, scientific world-views do not fundamentally conflict with Christianity, properly understood. It was believed that theology must 'mediate' and 'correlate' between the two worlds of reason and revelation in order to show how the modern believer can inhabit both worlds, religious and secular, with integrity (Graham, Walton and Ward, 2005: 138–69).

A new generation of theologians came to prominence during the 1990s, however, who were not interested in such accommodation or correlation (Hauerwas and Wells, 2004; Milbank, Ward and Pickstock, 1999; Milbank, 1990). They aim to correct what they see as a fundamental error of modern, liberal theology, which was to surrender ground to secular standards of scientific 'objectivity' and reason. These critics of mainstream public theology argue that to enter the public domain or debate in a secular society is already to have surrendered to the view that Christianity is one view among many, and thus to capitulate to a form of relativism. They argue that the future for theology is to root itself in ecclesiology – the life of the church – not in accommodation to generic humanist discourse. This is often termed a 'post-liberal' perspective, since it rejects the precepts of liberal modernity that there are universal norms of reason and public debate to which we all subscribe: 'Only when the songs of Zion are sung for their own sake will they be sung well enough to gain currency in society at large' (Lindbeck, 1989: 54).

What is truthful, what is good, cannot be demonstrated by abstract principle, graspable by anyone of good character or rational intellect. It is about the ideals that a particular community subscribes to, the stories it tells, the living examples it produces; in the way a community 'performs' or lives out a vision of 'the good life' – or the good city. The church is the place where such virtues are cultivated: it has definitive narratives in Scripture; it has exemplary practices in its sacramental worship; it has a vision of a restored human community in the transforming death and resurrection of Jesus. A community that lives out this radical ethic cannot have anything to do with the compromises of secular reason. Instead, the church becomes the alternative 'public', as a fully authentic community that speaks for itself. Its own praxis is its own testimony; but it seeks neither to justify itself in terms of wider publics, nor to influence their discourses. God is only known through Jesus Christ who is more than a representative figure of humanity's highest virtues: he is rather the living Word that radically moulds and transforms the world. Christians 'participate' in God's community of peace and justice; the church is a 'sanctified' people. The way it treats the stranger, the weak, the disabled is a parable of God's Kingdom (Hauerwas, 1981).

In an age of secularisation, theologians such as those associated with 'radical orthodoxy' have proclaimed themselves 'post-secular' (Smith, 2004). They simply refuse to accept the premises of modernity's separation of the sacred from the secular or the privatisation of religion. Radical orthodoxy uses the (very complex) methods and vocabulary of cultural and literary studies to expose the emptiness and redundancy of secular post-modernity, pointing towards a need to reinstate the 'sacred' in the midst of social theory (Milbank, 1990). It appeals to the critical theories of postmodernism (poststructuralism, deconstruction, post-colonialism, critical theory) and their questioning of the 'grand narratives' (or sacred cows?) of modernity (humanism, reason, relativism, separation of sacred and secular, autonomy of secular knowledge). Postmodernism signals an end to 'foundational' truth, because it exposes the contingency and constructedness of all truth-claims.

Radical orthodoxy seizes the opportunity for theology to rediscover its own (transcendent, confessional) premises and argues that Christianity is freed from any obligation to explain itself to secular thought, but is able thereby to 'out-narrate' it. Radical orthodoxy offers a powerful vision of the Christian community as the place in which Christ's forgiveness and reconciliation is to be enacted, and to which it turns for its social ethics. The church is, as Milbank says, 'a new social body which can transgress every human boundary, and adopts no law in addition to that of "life" ... [and] is attendant upon a diverse yet harmonious, mutually reconciling community' (Milbank, 1990: 100).

Graham Ward's *Cities of God* (2000) is probably the best book in urban theology since *The Secular City* to take urban theory (questions of 'what makes a city?' 'what makes a *good* city?') seriously. But *contra* Harvey Cox, Ward's city is a fragmented, atomised and deeply troubled place. For example, Ward offers an extended analysis of the formlessness of cyber-space as the epitome of this rootlessness: the fantasy-like nature of virtual reality renders all meaning superficial and fragile; nothing seems to have depth or durability. Similarly, he considers how much of consumerism – and in particular pornography – promises the satisfaction of all desires unimpeded by material limitations. This is, for Ward, an unacceptable denial of humanity's basic finitude, perpetuated by Enlightenment ideas of progress, perfectibility and mastery of nature. However, secular modernity is incapable of articulating the very foundations on which its ultimate values rest: 'only theology can give to secularism a legitimacy that saves it from nihilistic self-consumption' (2000: 236). So in keeping with the reversals of radical orthodoxy over Protestant liberalism, we see how it is the secular that is now reliant on theology to remind it of its true vocation, not the other way around. But radical orthodoxy is not simply a restate-ment of 'tradition' that repudiates secular values. Rather, it offers us a way of 'reading' cities like so many texts, enabling the chaotic and random signs that circulate in the urban to be reassembled into a coherent theological world-view.

Ward's city is, however, a very ethereal place, despite references to the streets of Manchester. Some of this is deliberate, in terms of its stress on the ubiquity of virtual reality and the fantasies of film, consumerism and pornography. Yet the reader looks in vain for the kind of empirical observations on the grass-roots stories of urban communities living with the material issues of poverty, drugs, crime, decaying infrastructure, mar-ginalisation, or community development such as characterised *Faith in the City*. Similarly, in keeping with post-liberalism and radical orthodoxy's 'idealism' concerning the church as herald of reconciliation, there is little attention to actual local churches' strategies for urban regeneration.

For the American scholar William Cavanaugh, the collapse of Christendom in the West and secularisation has meant an effacement of the church from history (Cavanaugh, 2003). Modernity is premised on a division between 'sacred' and 'secular'; the autonomy of secular reason and the neutrality of the public square. If religion and theological world-views want to gain entry to public debate or influence policy, therefore, they have to ask permission to conform to the rules of public discourse, which is wary of professions of faith, since it is built on its very exclusion. But for Cavanaugh, that is an attenuation of the church to the level of being just one voluntary organisation within civil society. With the end of Christendom, political and public theologies can only work at one remove, since they are dependent on understandings of public debate as premised on an ability to influence by reasoned argument, or by the role and activism of Christians as part of pluralist civil society.

Post-liberal theology refuses to collude with this division, however, since it is a capitulation to the division between sacred and secular that is now being challenged in the name of the resacralisation of the world and the resurgence of religion. Cavanaugh puts forward the alternative, which is to argue that the church is central to God's plan of salvation and 'bears the fullness of God's politics through history' (Cavanaugh, 2003: 403). Politics is the outworking of God's power, and the church is the embodiment of the way a transformative politics takes shape. It is what the church is, as a prefiguration of a new Jerusalem in its liturgical and devotional life, rather than how it writes reports on urban poverty or nurtures citizenship skills, that matters. 'The role of the church is not merely to make policy recommendations to the state, but to embody a different kind of politics, so that the world may be able to see a truthful politics and be transformed' (Cavanaugh, 2003: 404). This is not a refusal of the obligations of citizenship, however, but an attempt to assert a pattern of discipleship as primary and definitive. The signs by which Christians are incorporated into the *ekklesia* (which means assembly of citizens), such as baptism and Eucharist, are not just worship or spiritual exercises but acutely political, since they are acts of forming communities that are about proclaiming God's alternative rule of power in the form of the Kingdom. But the church doesn't waste time dealing with secular politics: it must concentrate on embodying that world to come. The church will ultimately prevail – even though its message is one of peace not triumphalism – and it is its own institutional life that provides the blueprint for the world's salvation.

Elsewhere, Cavanaugh describes how the Eucharist, a liturgical rite, can itself be a kind of public theology: 'a Christian practice of the political is embodied in the Eucharist' (1998: 2). This provides us with a clear illustration of how post-liberals identify the 'performance' of the church as the essence of its public life. Cavanaugh uses the example of the church in Chile, insisting that the church must intervene in opposing things like abuses of human rights, genocide and torture. Yet the task for public theology is not about issuing statements to say 'torture is bad' or lobbying the United Nations, or using a universal language of human rights. Rather, the church's resistance needs to be enacted, embodied and performed.

Torture is an attack on the human body, a specific person's physical being, and a means of reducing their bodily integrity into an object of violence, a means of extracting information or humiliating them. Since torture contains ritual elements, an 'alternative economy' or ritual of embodiment must be restored in its place: one that acknowledges the obscenity of torture, but which proclaims an alternative vision of embodiment that is redemptive. The body has been ritually instrumentalised and objectified, and in its place, says Cavanaugh, is a rite that proclaims 'the reappearance of social bodies capable of countering the atomizing performances of the State' (1998: 4). The Eucharist is a way of saying – not by speech or writing, but by symbol and sacrament – that death and torture do not have the final word. In the process it renders the church as the institutional bearer of resistance to state-sanctioned violence.

Critics of post-liberal theology

> While many political theologians applaud postliberal theology's defense of an evangelical form of ecclesial resistance to individualistic, bourgeois academic interpretations of Christianity, they also challenge the postliberal inclination to separate the spiritual and the political, lack of attention to justice issues, to critiques of ideology, and to action for ecclesial and social reforms. (Heyer, 2004: 324)

In its favour, the appeal of post-liberalism rests in its scepticism towards universal rationality, in favour of the celebration of the distinctiveness of a community set apart. However, many critics argue that this counter-cultural aspect and its refusal to play by the rules of the secular state means the church loses any foothold whatsoever in the public realm. In a milder form, this can be seen when many urban churches apply for external funding for projects and are faced with the choice between assimilation into external time-frames and outcomes and an ability to set their own agenda, albeit outside the 'mainstream'.

Similarly, if a public theology of the world needs to recover its roots in the church, then this post-liberal tradition may need to rediscover where a theology of the church reconnects with the real world. As Cavanaugh himself concedes, 'it is by no means always clear in practice where the boundaries of the church lie' (2003: 405). Critics often ask whether such utopian communities are possible, and whether they are capable of embodying such pristine separatism. The sociology of English religion has generally not been one of the gathered remnant, but of overlapping affinities between parish and people; and this does not simply reflect the vestiges of Establishment but the realities of Christian commitment, which is that people exercise discipleship alongside the everyday compromises of secular vocation. They cannot separate their calling as Christians from their lives as social workers, school governors, business people and police officers. In that respect, there is no pristine 'Christian witness' that is not in some sense shaped by its surrounding context.

We have seen the tensions between two different theologies of public life, therefore. One proceeds from a conviction that the precepts and teachings of the Christian tradition are reflected in the axioms of 'common wisdom', and that the task of the church is to commit itself to partnerships of many kinds. Alternatively, there are those who regard the Gospel as a more exclusive discourse that is designed to shape the distinctiveness of the community of faith and to erupt prophetically into a world forgetful of transcendence and the sacred: 'for one the task entails describing and living the Scriptural narrative authentically, and for the other it demands continually attempting to explain that narrative and its implications and relate them to experience and other knowledge' (Heyer, 2004: 325).

Augustine and the *City of God*

Is there a way of reconciling these strands? One classic reflection on the city, which perhaps serves more as a metaphor for the human condition, rather than emerging from empirical study, may provide a way forward. Yet it is significant for what we have said about theology emerging from practical matters that Augustine wrote his great treatise *City of God*

(413–27 CE) in response to a real political crisis: the fall of the city of Rome in 410 CE to the Northern European Goths, signalling the collapse of the Empire and an entire civilisation. Augustine by then was a bishop in Hippo in North Africa, but, like the rest of Europe, the Mediterranean and North Africa, he felt the shock-waves. In particular, he was aware of critics who attributed the fall of Rome to the adoption of Christianity as the official religion of the Empire under Constantine in 313 CE. People said that Rome had been weakened by turning away from its traditional gods and that the presence of Christians had introduced traitors into its midst: people whose ultimate loyalty was to their God, who, they argued, transcended and surpassed the authority of the earthly rule of the Emperor. Augustine set out, in part, to argue that a Christian political order was still a legitimate form of rule and that far from undermining healthy body politic, Christianity could be channelled into the good of the city.

Relevant to our concerns is the fact that Augustine was writing out of a complex and pluralistic social and cultural context. Although Christianity had been adopted as the official religion, this was still a complex world, with Christians living alongside pagans, Jews and marginal sects of their own such as the Gnostics and Manichaeans, as well as the Goths knocking at the gates of Rome. This was not the settled Christendom of medieval Europe but a real melting-pot; and perhaps, given the challenges of 'mainstream' liberal public theology in the face of the collapse of Christendom, we do well to remember that the 'public' into which Augustine intervened was also diverse, changing, multiple and contentious.

Augustine himself had a varied background: a man of the world as well as a man of God. He was an educated man, a successful official in the Roman civil service, raised not as a Christian, influenced in early years by Manichaeism, a sect of Christianity that believed in the division of the world into light and dark, good and evil. Like the Gnostics, the Manichaeans believed that the world of matter, nature and embodiment was corrupt, and the task of religion was to induct the believer into a divine world of reason and light. However, Augustine was converted to Christianity in 387, a journey he later recorded in another famous work, the *Confessions*.

The central idea in *City of God* is that of the two cities, a theme that renders Augustine's thought absolutely central for all forms of public and political theology. These two cities issue from humanity's conflicting desires: desire, or love of self (*amor sui v. fui*), and desire, or love of God (*amor dei v. fui*). The love of self is driven by self-interest, individualism, lust for power; the love of God is characterised by charity, generosity and a concern for the good of all. Augustine argues that these two visions or impulses co-exist not only in the hearts and minds of each individual, but in the way common or corporate life is managed.

Despite the tension, the struggle between these two cities, however, Augustine rejects the idea that love of God and love of world or self are incompatible. His is not a Manichaean world-view, arguing for the overcoming of the material, temporal world of flesh and history in favour of ascending to some ideal spiritual realm. Augustine argued that Christians must not abandon the challenge of living in the world as it is, even while they live in anticipation of the world to come. This is because of Augustine's doctrine of God, who is both transcendent and immanent: 'most high and most near, always absent and always present' (*Confessions*). In Christ, God became part of human history and shared our humanity; but through his death and resurrection, he has redeemed (fallen) creation and offered creaturely humanity a way of overcoming the love of self by virtue of their participation in the life of the risen Christ.

Charles Mathewes, in his book on Augustine and public theology (Mathewes, 2008), argues that for Augustine, sin is understood as 'privation' – like deprivation, an isolation of the self from the love of God – and is related to selfishness, or surrender to earthly desires. This is not just a question of being divorced from God, however, but from one's fellow creatures, the whole of nature; of not being capable of desiring their well-being and flourishing, and failing to see one's common destiny with them under God. For Augustine, redemption from that sin or privation entails a restoration of our very 'public-ity': a turning back to right relation with God, our neighbour, non-human nature, and so on. So the suggestion is, argues Mathewes, that redemption and a restoration of humanity's true purposes under the rule of *amor Dei* is necessarily a public state because it is about restoring the connections between all things.

However, this redemption, while having been inaugurated, has yet to be ultimately fulfilled. It has a question of 'now and not yet' about it. The important thing is that Christians are called to participate with Christ in the redemption of the world, by remaining in the world. It would be mistaken to believe, however, that Augustine conceived of these two cities as two separate places: as if one were the secular world of politics and the other the relative sanctuary of the church; or even as two contending political parties or manifestos.

William Cavanaugh provides a helpful metaphor for this when he returns to Augustine's idea of the 'city of God' to examine how Christians are to manage the balance between religious faith and public reason, the tensions of discipleship and citizenship. He describes the two realms not as separate self-contained worlds, but as almost virtual spaces, overlapping each other; but they are primarily performative spaces, in which different narratives (in our case of well-being and human fulfilment) are lived out.

> Envisioning the two cities as performances helps us to avoid some serious problems with the way the church is imagined. The church as God sees it – the Body of Christ – is not a human institution with well-defined boundaries, clearly distinguishable from the secular body politic. The church is not a *polis*, but a set of practices or performances that participate in the history of salvation that God is unfolding on earth ... The church is not a separate enclave, but ... it joins with others to perform the city of God. (Cavanaugh, 2006: 318)

Augustine's two cities are not the same as the 'two Kingdoms' of sacred and secular, where two sets of rules or language abide. It is rather about being in the world but not of the world: of affirming the goodness of creation while anticipating its further and ultimate transformation. For Augustine, it is about recognising humanity driven by selfish desires but also carrying the capacity to respond to the promptings of the divine within them. Neither require a withdrawal from temporal or secular affairs, however; rather, they demand something close to what the twentieth-century theologian Reinhold Niebuhr and his commentators were to call 'Realism' – a recognition that the world is both good and fallen, a faith that things will be transformed while aware that this will never be achieved by human efforts alone (R. Niebuhr, 1932). But the solution is not to despair or become over-confident, but to live with the tensions creatively and constructively.

So the two (metaphorical) cities express the provisionality of living in and yet between these two horizons. We participate in the world as it is, since creation is fully God's; and yet we are also aware that we are not to be totally assimilated or to fall prey to the illusion that it is permanent or God-given. Instead, Christians are called to await the interjection of divine grace into human affairs, which still means that public life is granted special sanction, since it becomes a way in which human beings can simultaneously involve themselves in the common life of the world and work for its transformation.

Augustine offers some important themes that are very helpful for approaching the task of articulating a public, urban theology that is mindful of the twin vocations of citizenship and discipleship. We have already argued for a tension in contemporary public theology between affirming that of God in all people and seeking the common good beyond the boundaries of its own teaching in the name of a shared humanity and a common political project, versus the alternative of a Christian identity rooted in its own tradition in such a way that it retains a distinctiveness about its very contribution. Slip one way and it risks simply 'baptising' or endorsing the status quo; slip the other and it loses its public-ity – its ability to speak in any common language, to seek affinities despite superficial differences. But possibly Augustine, writing about the nature of Christian identity and witness within the complex Roman body politic – the urban reminds contemporary theology of that being a necessary tension, constituting the very heart of theological reality out of which public theology must work.

We can find this very synthesis in the work of a theologian such as Thomas Aquinas, for example. For Aquinas, the world of nature and intellectual enquiry held the potential to lead people to God; but while they may betray 'some sort of trace of a likeness to God', human reason is still restricted, unschooled, weak. So the guiding hand of tradition was still necessary; since God is essentially mystery, not to be discerned by human efforts but by the gift of grace. Yet much of his major work, *Summa Theologiae*, sets out to show that arguments for the existence of God can be conducted using logic, observation, argument and deduction. Similarly, later Protestant theologians such as John Calvin and Abraham de Kuyper come to talk about 'common grace'. This is the notion that while there may be specific and unique revelation through the tradition – and for Christians, specifically in the person and work of Christ – God has also created other means by which others might be drawn to glimpse salvation: reason, a human striving for truth. Furthermore, Christians – like all theists – believe that God is bigger than human consciousness, and transcends both our finitude and any particular human or cultural expression of truth. That means awareness of the good or the divine can never be limited to one single means of revelation, since God acts independent of human efforts. For public theologians of this mainstream liberal tradition, the significance it grants to human reason, scientific enquiry, non-Christian expressions of virtue, is derived from this conviction that God acts in nature and grace as well as revelation. 'In Christ we are offered the possibility of partaking in the reality of God and in the reality of the world, but not in the one without the other. The reality of God discloses itself only by setting me entirely in the reality of the world ...' (Bonhoeffer, 1995: 193).

Conclusion

The history of urban life and faith, and thus to a large extent of theological thinking about the nature of our cities and the church's role within them, has since the Industrial Revolution been shaped by a narrative of the decline of religious observance and the gradual marginalisation of religious institutions, not least mainstream denominations such as the Church of England. Yet while formal religious affiliation in the West did show signs of decline throughout the nineteenth and twentieth centuries, the consensus now is that the evidence for such decline may well have been over-emphasised, and that the last quarter of the twentieth century to the present day is marked by the emergence of heterodox and pluralist forms of religious practice and organisation – some the result of global migration, some to do with a greater freedom to experiment with diverse expressions of personal spirituality – which suggest that faith has not disappeared from our cities. Yet as is already becoming clear, this cannot signal a return to traditional forms of ecclesial or theological conduct as if the tides of the sea of faith have not dramatically receded. As we argued in our discussion of the nature of theology in the public realm, this is not about a return to Christendom and 'business as usual' for the Established Church. Rather, it is about a quest for a reformulated public theology that is adequate to address the complexities of urban life and faith, with all its contradictory currents of secularism and re-enchantment. While some of the preoccupations of theology of the past may seem anachronistic, they have much to teach us about how people responded to the crises of their own context and how we might inherit some of their wisdom in charting our own journeys of citizenship and discipleship.

2
Urban Theology as Public Theology

We continue our theological reflection on the urban church with a consideration of the way various church reports have approached the topic. We focus in particular on two major reports from the past twenty-five years *Faith in the City* (ACUPA, 1985) and *Faithful Cities* (CULF, 2006) – which serve as illuminating case studies into some of the dimensions of *public theology* that we set out in Chapter 1. These two reports, and others like them, have sought to comment on the changing nature of our towns and cities through the lenses of Christian faith, and thereby to contribute a theologically informed voice to public policy. In some cases, they have had a considerable impact on government and public policy in communicating something of the realities of urban life and faith to a wider public audience. *Faith in the City*, a seminal work in the history of Anglican social thought, begins to demonstrate, as we will argue, one of the unique characteristics of the Church of England's contribution to urban life and faith: its emphasis on the primacy of the local congregation and the (seemingly paradoxical) value of Establishment as a conduit for engaging church and state, and of linking local experience with national debate.

As well as reflecting the realities of urban life and shaping public perception, these reports have also attempted, in different ways and with varying degrees of success, to enable the church itself to reflect theologically on the particular challenges facing urban Christians in their everyday lives and callings. By tracing some of the milestones in the development of public theology in and about the urban context, we therefore hope to offer further insight into the way urban contexts serve as places of learning and renewed theological understanding. Yet an overview of the past twenty or

thirty years of public theology also prompts the question of whether such a vision can actually make a difference to public perceptions and government policy. Indeed, it may be that the story of the journey from *Faith in the City* to *Faithful Cities* and beyond is one of irrevocable erosion in the credibility of such church-sponsored interventions into public life, with corresponding implications for the very project of public theology itself.

Our main emphasis in this chapter will be on our shared experience of involvement in the Archbishops' Commission on Urban Life and Faith (CULF), which produced the report *Faithful Cities*, published in May 2006. It was, after all, as a result of *Faithful Cities* that Stephen was appointed Bishop for Urban Life and Faith, with particular responsibility to follow up its main recommendations, work which has contributed in large part to the writing of this book. As well as examining the report itself, therefore, we will trace some of the ways in which the concerns of CULF continue to attract debate in church and nation alike.

We will begin, however, by locating that report in a 20-year history of urban theology that began with the seminal report *Faith in the City*, published in 1985, and which is considered by many to represent the high watermark of twentieth-century public theology in the UK. While *Faith in the City* was ground-breaking, many of its conclusions and theological presuppositions now seem less relevant to changing times, an insight that strongly shaped CULF's self-understanding. The themes of continuity and change over the two decades between these landmark reports therefore run throughout our discussion, and we conclude with some of the chief priorities for public theology in relation to urban life and faith to have emerged overall.

Faith in the City **and beyond**

One piece of public theology dominates recent urban theology within the Anglican context – *Faith in the City*, the report of the Archbishop's Commission on Urban Priority Areas, appointed in 1981 (ACUPA, 1985). It has been the subject of much examination and debate (Henry Clark, 1993; Harvey, 1989; Graham, 1996) and, in the shape of initiatives such as the Church Urban Fund, contributed much in the way of shaping current practice. The immediate catalyst to *Faith in the City* was the outbreak of disturbances in a number of inner-city areas in the summer of 1981. In 1982, under pressure from urban bishops concerned about inner-city problems such as unemployment, breakdown of community relations with police, denigration of housing stock and other infrastructure, cuts in social services, education and local amenities, the then Archbishop of Canterbury, Robert Runcie, announced the appointment of a commission on the plight of urban areas.

Its original terms of reference were: 'To examine the strengths, insights, problems and needs of the Church's life and mission in Urban Priority Areas and, as a result, to reflect on the challenge which God may be making to Church and Nation: and to make recommendations to appropriate bodies' (ACUPA, 1985: iii). Its intentions to fulfil a particular kind of public role are immediately evident. The terminology of 'commission' is revealing in its adoption of the terminology of government-sponsored 'royal commissions' that had been seminal in shaping public opinion and formulating public policy in Britain on matters such as public health, education and factory reform throughout the nineteenth and twentieth centuries. It is interesting to note that the Conservative Government under Margaret Thatcher in all its eleven years of office (1979–90) never appointed a single royal commission of its own. For some, this reflected the Government's determination to reduce the power of the state and the influence of an independent civil society in favour of a commitment to minimalist government and the power of the market.

With a chairperson, Sir Richard O'Brien, a high-ranking civil servant who had been head of the Manpower Services Commission, and other members from trade unions, industry, the voluntary sector, education as well as the churches, the Commission had the feel of a senior arm of the civil service. Yet at the same time as locating itself within the processes of governance – albeit from a non-governmental position – ACUPA also stressed the significance of a local, grass-roots focus. Commissioners carried out a series of visits to urban priority areas, something that gave its members first-hand experience, and that proved a source of invaluable evidence, especially in the face of criticism of the final report as politically motivated. Arguably, it reflects two emphases that are consistently characteristic of Anglican social thought, the first of which is to value the importance of engaging with empirical evidence (Henry Clark, 1993: 73); and the second – potentially more innovative and more radical – is to pay attention to grass-roots communities and to receive and value voices and perspectives which often did not find their way into the public domain. This gave the report an authenticity and immediacy that its critics found hard to refute, and that underlines the significance of local knowledge and engagement for such a public theology:

> We decided from the outset that we must spend some time in the UPAs to see for ourselves the human reality behind the official statistics. In the course of a series of visits we saw something of the physical conditions under which people in the UPAs are living, and we listened to their own accounts and experiences at open public meetings and in smaller invited groups. We also spent many hours with representatives of local government, the police, social workers, the various caring agencies and the local churches themselves. (ACUPA, 1985: xiv)

Faith in the City was published in December 1985. It delivered an uncompromising attack on the Conservative Government of Margaret Thatcher, which it believed was worsening the plight of areas affected by the economic downturn by restricting state expenditure on social services, education and income support in the interests of doctrinaire monetarist policies. *Faith in the City* also underlined the critical importance of the church's presence in urban priority areas at a time when government, business and others were abandoning them.

The Commission concluded that the state of the cities was a critical indicator of the extent to which Britain could call itself a just and equitable society. Yet in its final paragraph the report adopts a different tone and speaks not of public policy so much as the personal journey undertaken by the commissioners:

> each of us has faced a personal challenge to our lives and life styles: a call to change our thinking and action in such a way as to help us to stand more closely alongside the risen Christ with those who are poor and powerless. We have found faith in the city. (ACUPA, 1985: 360)

In extending that call to the whole of the church to stand in solidarity with marginalised urban communities, the report set in train a concerted strategy of deploying staff and resources in urban priority areas. Under the auspices of the Church Urban Fund, money was redistributed within the church, and external funding generated to support a range of major projects in local areas. In the years that followed, the mainstream Christian denominations produced a series of reports on the state of urban priority areas (ACAGUPA, 1990; Methodist Church, 1997; Cooper, 1992; Harvey, 1989). As the twentieth century drew to a close, however, and especially after the election of the New Labour Government in 1997, it was clear that the social and economic context in which the urban church was operating had substantially altered. Twenty years on from ACUPA, the church was faced with the task of addressing the altogether more ambivalent trends of urban regeneration in the early years of the twenty-first century. The physical and economic landscape of our cities had changed out of all recognition. Increasingly, a mood of antagonism to government was being replaced by a context of partnership, beginning with the Conservatives' regeneration initiatives in the early 1990s and continuing with the election of New Labour in 1997. The Methodist report, *The Cities*, published in 1997, contains a digest of the various regeneration initiatives undertaken by Conservative and Labour Governments since 1990, which showed that *Faith in the City*'s analysis of a government policy of non-intervention and neglect of urban areas could now not be further from the truth (Methodist Church, 1997).

Indeed, by the early 2000s formerly depressed and decaying cities such as Liverpool, Manchester and Newcastle were vibrant hubs of regional economic renewal, largely prompted by a proliferation of government-sponsored regeneration measures which often involved strategic partnerships with the voluntary and community sectors and business (Steele, 2009). As critics have noted, *Faith in the City*'s call for comprehensive reinvestment on the part of central government into social services and local infrastructure – essentially, a return to a model of tax-funded, centrally delivered state welfare – was already an anachronism by 1985, but it had well and truly been superseded by the economic upturn in most major English cities by the beginning of the twenty-first century. It was time for a reappraisal on the part of the churches, if not of their commitment to urban priority areas, then to the changing nature of the urban economy and in particular to a phenomenon known as 'urban regeneration'.

Into this context, and with the twentieth anniversary of *Faith in the City* approaching, came an influential paper from the Church of England Urban Bishops' Panel, published in 2002. It attempted to address the changing economic and social landscape of English towns and cities and to elaborate on the nature of the church's task. It argued that if the churches (and especially the Church of England) were committed to maintaining a long-term presence in urban areas, it needed a more proactive and strategic understanding of its own mission and ministry. Keeping faith with the city required a willingness 'to address deep rooted [sic] situations, as well as [to] engage directly and consistently with change as it happens in our society' (2002: 6). The report also identified the emergence of a veritable regeneration 'industry', which epitomised the sea-change from *Faith in the City*, while remarking on its aspirational vocabulary that drew startlingly on theological imagery and the language of spirituality: 'The language of renewal, regeneration and renaissance speak of the spiritual dimension to the reordering of our cities. It is language which belongs to the theological categories by which the Church witnesses to God's involvement in and concern for every aspect of human life' (Urban Bishops' Panel, 2002: 23).

Faithful Cities: celebration, vision, justice

The Commission for Urban Life and Faith was appointed in February 2004, with the objective to 'discern and promote a positive vision of urban society and the churches' presence and witness within it' (http://www.culf.org/sections/panda). It comprised thirteen contributing members, plus consultants, a secretariat and additional contributors. Its report *Faithful Cities: a call for celebration, vision and justice* was launched in May 2006.

Some of the findings of *Faithful Cities* may be summarised as follows. An early chapter, 'Continuity and Change', attempted an evaluation of the main changes that have occurred since the 1980s and since the publication of *Faith in the City*. 'The World in our Cities' identified as one of the most significant changes a substantial increase in ethnic and religious diversity within our cities (CULF, 2006: 17–29). 'Prosperity: In Pursuit of Well-being' highlighted the persistence of marked inequalities in income, health, education and housing, despite the very real successes of urban regeneration (2006: 30–44). For many in our cities, the quality of life had not improved, and increases in wealth had not necessarily led to greater levels of reported happiness. Young people in particular appeared to experience high levels of insecurity and depression. 'Regeneration for People: More than Status, Power and Profit' questioned the long-term sustainability of regeneration programmes, noting the rise in gated communities and the resulting exclusion of the poorest from city centres and affordable housing (2006: 54–65). 'A Good City: Urban Regeneration with People in Mind' looks at how regeneration can make cities healthy and happy places to live. 'Involved and Committed' argues for the positive and distinctive contribution of faith-based organisations to the welfare of their local neighbourhoods in the shape of a commodity it calls 'faithful capital' (2006: 66–75). Overall, the report exposed critical gaps between the rhetoric and reality of regeneration, by pointing to the stubborn persistence of deep-rooted inequalities of income and opportunity beneath the facade of prosperity, and by interrogating the very visions and values underpinning the ambitions of such initiatives.

Faithful Cities concluded with eleven recommendations, some aimed at the Church of England and other churches and faith communities; others at the Government and the voluntary sector. The report called on the Church of England to maintain a 'planned, continued and substantial' presence in urban areas and to ensure that church leaders, lay and ordained, are given training in urban and contextual theology. Churches should look to their own attitudes to wealth and poverty to ensure that members' lifestyles are not selfish or exploitative of others, globally or locally. The Government was asked to consider setting a 'living' wage rather than the statutory minimum wage, and to tackle the gap between those living in poverty and the very wealthy. It was challenged to 'lead rather than follow' public opinion on immigration, refugee and asylum policy, allowing asylum-seekers to find paid work to support themselves. Faith groups must combat racism, fascism and religious intolerance and promote networks of understanding and engagements within and between faith groups. The reconstruction of the Youth Service must be a priority, with both faith communities and government giving attention to the informal education and spiritual well-being of young people. The Church Urban Fund should continue to be supported, and a national debate about 'What makes a good city?' should be initiated by church leaders on a wide-ranging basis.

In her evaluation of *Faithful Cities*, Ruth McCurry, a member of the original ACUPA, notes a number of contrasts in style and tone which sum up the differences between *Faith in the City* and *Faithful Cities* (McCurry, 2007). She argues that while this is to be expected given the passage of time, it is also indicative of significant differences between the two Commissions and how they viewed their respective tasks. She notes that ACUPA undertook first-hand observation of urban priority areas, whereas CULF was more theoretical.[2] CULF certainly attempted to let local voices and testimonies speak, but these narratives often sit uncomfortably along-side the more analytical text of the main report. *Faithful Cities* is busy, cluttered and colourful, in contrast to *Faith in the City*'s sober prose. One of Elaine's colleagues remarked to her at the Manchester launch of *Faithful Cities* that whereas *Faith in the City* reminded him of a government White Paper, *Faithful Cities* was more like the annual report of a voluntary organisation! That difference may be more than superficial, however, since the difference in styles reflects the changing social and religious context in which the two Commissions worked. ACUPA spoke to 'church and nation' with confidence, in the belief that its legacy of Establishment would guarantee that its findings would find easy correspondence with mainstream public opinion. It speaks, even, of 'those basic Christian principles of justice and compassion which we believe we share with the great majority of the people of Britain' (ACUPA, 1985: xiv). As McCurry points out, however, ACUPA drew from trade unions, the civil service, the public sector and social policy, as well the churches, whereas CULF drew its membership much less extensively from secular employment. The result is that '*Faithful Cities* reads as a report largely of concern to those working in the churches in urban areas' (McCurry, 2007: 40). Perhaps *Faithful Cities* was simply a much more 'churchy' report, but at the time the membership of CULF felt challenged to identify the vantage point from which it spoke. At a time of declining religious influence in society and increasing cultural pluralism, it was not felt possible to adopt an authoritative Christian public voice. How, then, was a church-based commission to speak and command public attention?

The vantage point from which CULF would speak was thus uppermost in members' minds. In addition, one of the criticisms levelled at *Faith in the City* had precisely been its lack of sustained theological reflection to inform its findings. It was quite possible to read the report without engaging with its theological chapter and not losing the thread of the argument. Yet, especially since CULF could not assume that its audience would share its core convictions, it was adamant to make the connections between theology and practice more apparent. How was it to do that without retreating into specialist language, or appearing to preach to the nation? In other words, what were the premises of this piece of 'public theology' to be?

The decision was made that the theological basis of CULF's argument must be declared not as a statement of doctrinal or ecclesial exclusivity, but as a profession of faith that informed its analysis and conclusions yet was also open and transparent about its origins. In other words, as *Faithful Cities* argues, this is an authentically 'public' theology that is prepared to defend the foundations of its own principles while ensuring that its own internal discourse is accessible and comprehensible to a wider constituency: 'While theology provides the vocabulary of faithful action, it can never be the language of a sectarian few, and it should be prepared to engage critically and constructively with alternative points of view' (CULF, 2006: 15, 2.65).

Not content with simply a socio-economic analysis of the state of our cities, *Faithful Cities* was therefore at pains to offer a theologically grounded critique of urban life and faith. It was intended to emphasise that the actions of the urban church and its membership were essentially rooted in what it professed about the nature of God, even though it was concerned to promote the common good of all members of the community, and to work in partnership with those of all faiths and none. Similarly, CULF's critique of programmes of urban regeneration, and the vision of the long-term renewal and well-being of our cities that these represented, would also be based on theologically derived values of justice, equity and human dignity, even though many of those would overlap with broader traditions.

The Commission therefore took the decision to 'front-load' its theology with a statement of the axioms on which its evaluation of urban life is grounded:

- God is the source of all life and gives purpose and character to all of creation.
- As a consequence of being made in the image and likeness of God, all human beings share 'an innate and irreducible dignity'.
- Humanity's deepest fulfilment is to be found in relationships of 'mutuality, love and justice' which are derived from our original calling into relationship with God. (2006: 2)

Another theological issue preoccupied us from the start, and that was the significance of theologies of liberation for the Commission. *Faith in the City* had, notoriously, used motifs from liberation theology in its theological chapter, leading to some accusations of 'Marxism' from its detractors. Elaine has argued for a number of years that this is to misunderstand the intentions of the authors of *Faith in the City*. They used liberationist analysis as a way of calling the church to regard the Gospel as concerned with structural injustices and not simply with personal morality, rather than intentionally adopted Marxist economic or social analysis (Graham, 1996; CULF, 2006: 14, 2.52–3). However, the emergence of liberation theology – which is, after all, historically a movement of the urban poor – was also political in its stress on empowerment, being a theology 'from the underside of history', putting the Bible into the hands of ordinary Christians, valuing the experiences of those at the grass roots and exercising God's 'preferential option for the poor'. In the faces of the poor, we glimpse the face of Christ. *Faithful Cities* therefore concluded that it was a theological imperative to exercise solidarity with the most vulnerable, but also to see them and their experiences and contexts as valuable sources of theological understanding.

> In our enquiries ... we have emphasized the stories, insights and experiences that emerge from urban communities of faith. We have tried to be attentive to what these understandings may have to say to the world at large ... We have called these 'everyday theologies' referring to the popular, the language of the streets, the vernacular, or ... 'ordinary theology' ... We are therefore looking for signs of new liturgies and expressions of spirituality ... which speak more authentically from, and to, the lives of those in our urban areas. (CULF, 2006: 15: 2.61–3)

If *Faith in the City* adopted an economic advocacy for urban priority areas, *Faithful Cities* was concerned to extend that into a theological advocacy: it endorsed the ability of ordinary, grass-roots, poorly resourced congregations and communities to name their own experiences as holy and to see God at work around them, and to give that expression in their own 'vernacular' words of prayer, worship and spirituality. For some members of the Commission, this meant giving particular attention to the way in which young people might find spiritual meaning in forms of popular culture, of listening to those at the grass roots and of paying testimony to the vitality of expressions of faith they found at the margins. It also meant that the published report attempted to embody the narrative approach of the report in its printed format, by combining paragraphs of analysis with pictures and text boxes of narrative and case studies. These reflected a desire to integrate the voices that are often marginalised by official accounts – be

it the 'top-down' and deadline-driven agendas of regeneration programmes or even the institutional church – and to let them speak.

For many readers of the report, however, the juxtaposition of colourful
text boxes and substantive text succeeded more in interrupting the flow of
argument than in integrating the different stylistic registers of local stories,
socio-economic analysis and theological and biblical themes. The root
problem may be one of editorial coherence, although it may also point to a
more deep-rooted question of whether such aspirations towards faithful
representation of informal, grass-roots experience can ever be authentically achieved. It may be impossible to expect an 'official' report or
publication such as this ever to do justice to the spirituality of the urban
poor, or whether such opportunities can ever be contrived. The possibility
of advocacy by the powerful on behalf of the powerless, a theme present in
many theologies of liberation and close to the heart of many in the urban
church, remains unresolved, although we shall return to the theme of
empowerment in Chapter 7.

While *Faithful Cities* is bullish in its evaluation of the continuing
significance of religion and the contribution of faith-based organisations to
public life, it is at pains to avoid any suggestion that Britain is experiencing
a religious revival. The continuing decline in institutional Christianity
throughout Europe and certainly in the UK is undeniable, although much
current debate in the sociology of religion is focused on the extent to
which religion endures as a vestigial but influential cultural force through
disaffiliated forms of religious practices and new spiritualities (Garnett et
al., 2006), and how decline is tempered by the growth of British Islam and
the vitality of some minority Christian groups due to the presence of
migrants from Africa, the Caribbean and Eastern Europe. Yet CULF felt
itself to be witnessing contradictory trends. There is a new prominence of
matters of faith within the public sphere, not just in the rhetoric of
individual politicians and the processes of government policy, but as
religion influences aspects of law, economics, welfare and citizenship.
Despite the continued existence of national established churches in England and Scotland, however, the nature of British public debate has tended
to fight shy of 'doing God' in public, a diffidence that extends throughout
the political culture. So, on the one hand, *Faithful Cities* acknowledged that
the 'notion that the Church has the right to speak about anything on
anyone's behalf is now open to question' (CULF, 2006: 8, 2.16); but, on
the other, it insisted on the enduring contribution of the 'moral sense' of

people of faith in all its manifestations, 'which proves such a potent source of transformation of individuals and neighbourhoods' (2006: 81, 8.18).

Poverty and prosperity

Another major thesis of *Faithful Cities* concerned the benefits of urban regeneration, which were considerable but still not universal. While extensive regeneration schemes in our cities have transformed their local economies and provided new opportunities for local communities, they have often exacerbated, rather than relieved, inequalities of wealth and income (CULF, 2006: 31–2, 4.1–16). A major difference between now and the 1980s is that poverty is likely to be due to low wages rather than unemployment, with many vulnerable to chronic levels of debt (2006: 35–6, 4.29–31). As far as the physical regeneration of our cities in terms of housing is concerned, the poorest members of urban communities have been neglected or priced out of their own neighbourhoods as the gentrification of urban environments has pushed them to the margins (2006: 61, 6.40, 46–7, 5.9–13).

Yet even the achievements of economic regeneration for those who reap the benefits have their shadow side. A growing body of significant research across a range of disciplines suggests that growing material prosperity in Western countries does not necessarily produce greater happiness or well-being (Layard, 2005; James, 2007; Graham, 2009b). As *Faithful Cities* and other studies published since, such as that from the New Economics Foundation (Michaelson et al., 2009), have concluded, material signs of regeneration and prosperity need to be augmented by less tangible but nevertheless significant indicators: good personal and emotional relationships, strong links into a wider community, freedom to influence the course of one's life and a philosophy of life that extends beyond the fulfilment of one's own individual needs (CULF, 2006: 42).[3]

Since the publication of *Faithful Cities*, this question has become more prominent, and further research has added to CULF's intuition that indicators of subjective well-being should be taken very seriously as a measure of a nation's economic success and viability. Research by the Children's Society suggests that despite the UK's ranking as the fourth largest economy in the world, young people in Britain are among the most depressed in Europe (Layard and Dunn, 2009). The New Economics Foundation conducted a comprehensive survey of European countries during 2006–07, producing qualitative and quantitative measurements of 'personal' and 'social' well-being. Even before the advent of world recession, it concludes, there was a mismatch between people's expectations about what economic success was capable of delivering and their actual lived experience:

> Modern society is organised around a particular model of how to pursue human well-being. Baldly stated, this model contends that increasing economic output leads straightforwardly to improved well-being: a higher standard of living and a better quality of life across society. Economies are organised explicitly around the need to increase GDP, with relatively little regard for how it is distributed; business models are predicated on maximising profits to shareholders; and people are led to believe that the more disposable income they have – and thus the more they consume – the happier they will be. But economic indicators tell us nothing about whether people are in fact experiencing their lives as going well. There is a pressing need for a better, more direct way to measure society's performance against its overarching goal of improving well-being. (Michaelson et al., 2009: 13–14)

NEF does not incorporate religious affiliation into any of its variables when considering what factors influence individuals' and societies' experience – not an omission that North American research tends to make (Graham, 2009b: 11–12). Yet in suggesting that involvement in activities and organisations which furnish their members with strong social bonds and nurture intrinsic and resilient personal values, the report links with other research, especially social capital theory, which has pointed to religious participation as particularly rich in these respects. NEF identifies a number of axioms which, if appropriately promoted, might enhance personal and social well-being; the list reflects many of the virtues and practices cultivated by religious belief and belonging:

> *Connect*: ... Survey research has found that well-being is increased by life goals associated with family, friends, social and political life and decreased by goals associated with career success and material gains ... *Take notice*: ... research has shown that practising awareness of sensations, thoughts and feelings can improve both the knowledge we have about ourselves and our well-being for several years ...

Keep learning: ... Behaviour directed by personal goals to achieve something new has been shown to increase reported life satisfaction ...

Give: ... co-operative behaviour activates reward areas of the brain, suggesting we are hard wired to enjoy helping one another. Individuals actively engaged in their communities report higher well-being and their help and gestures have knock-on effects for others. (Michaelson et al., 2009: 46)

The question of what criteria adequately encapsulate our appreciation of the good life leads us back to another staple theme of *Faithful Cities* and a central plank of its methodology. It concerns the very criteria by which a successful or thriving city might be judged, the measures of virtue by which the *good* city is to be recognised.

The 'good city'

A modest but profound question runs throughout *Faithful Cities*: 'What makes a good city?' It is deceptively simple, yet served to do much to focus and promote the debate before and since. In some ways, it is reminiscent of the 'middle axioms' favoured by theologians and ethicists such as William Temple, J. H. Oldham and Ronald Preston in the middle decades of the twentieth century. Middle axioms inhabit the middle ground between general principles and specific policies, synthesised from the interaction of empirical facts and moral precepts, intended to be indicative statements of common wisdom rather than prescriptive manifestos. They are widely seen as one way in which the specific doctrines of the Christian tradition can be mediated into public policy. For Temple, middle axioms were sentiments such as 'freedom, social fellowship and service'; but just as middle axioms were intended to hold together a common discourse from which specific practical policies might emerge, so too might we see 'What makes a good city?' as an invitation to anyone, regardless of their personal faith or philosophy, to participate in an exchange of what matters most to them, and in the process to excavate the fundamental visions that might inform specific strategies for change and renewal.

As has already been indicated, the conclusion of *Faithful Cities* regarding the good city is concerned with equity, empowerment and participation (CULF 2006: 4, 1.26). In its emphasis on the non-material dimensions of the good city, however, it found some unexpected allies, in the shape of a generation of urban theorists, such as planners, sociologists and geographers, who were eschewing rationalist, forensic and quantitative analyses in favour of 'insurgent', narrative and holistic approaches.

Some members of the Commission had been greatly influenced by a new wave of urban geographers and planners, such as Nigel Thrift, Ash Amin, Doreen Massey and Leonie Sandercock, who challenged the rationalism and reductionism of modernist urban planning in favour of a bottom-up, grass-roots approach, in which participatory models of urban design and community development are preferred to the centralised, technocratic planning of an earlier generation. Andrew Davey has recently highlighted the strongly ethical and utopian tenor of much of this writing, and the growing convergence between the 'performative theology' of urban churches and the 'performative urbanisms' of new social movements. Both trends celebrate embodiment and imagination, the importance of localism and the forging of networks of 'openness and mutuality' into genuinely popular movements and alliances for social change, 'as alternative tellings of the city are acted out and glimpses of these visions made possible' (Davey, 2008: 43).

Although she is a secular humanist, Leonie Sandercock has written extensively about the 'spiritual' dimension to such a vision, drawing upon the insurgent struggles of indigenous and first peoples in Australia and Canada, for whom the sacredness of land becomes the expression of oppositional values based on the sanctity and integrity of the natural environment, the memory of place, the politics of vision and the practice of hope (Sandercock, 2003; CULF, 2006: 62, 6.50). This valuing of the non-material, the non-quantifiable, rings true with much of what *Faithful Cities* is seeking to affirm about the distinctiveness of a faith-based engagement, but Sandercock's vision is also one of 're-sacralising' the city:

> Perhaps we need a different way of talking about planning, but rather to recognize that spirituality may be embodied in planning work, whether we care to name it or not. But there may be some real purpose in naming it. It would mean a different way of seeing ourselves, representing ourselves to the world, and it would necessarily lead to different ways of teaching, which we might begin to think of as 'educating the heart' ... I think of spirituality as a way of being as well as a way of knowing, informed by certain values that then underpin ways of acting. (Sandercock, 2006: 66)

It was this kind of urban praxis which prompted us to insist on the importance of transcending the statistical and target-driven accounts of the good city to value the meanings and stories people invest in their actual inhabitation of space and place. It was also a way of registering the deeper questions of value necessary for the underpinning of urban regeneration strategies, and the importance of faith perspectives in fuelling such debates rather than simply sponsoring mere delivery of services:

> [S]trategies for regeneration frequently coalesce around four key principles of a good or successful city: (1) economics, (2) environment and infrastructure, (3) politics and governance and (4) culture. These four 'pillars of regeneration' relate to questions of physical resources, wealth-creation, sustainability and political structures. What they don't do is to take into account less quantifiable questions such as quality of life, wellbeing – happiness even – what we might term the 'human face' of the city. We have to ask questions about the *soul* of the city as well, and how faith communities can help develop this. (2006: 5)

Thus, *Faithful Cities* asks, 'What implicit values underpin strategies of regeneration in our major cities today? Is there a secular doctrine of salvation at work ...? Where are the signs of the transcendent in our cities?' (CULF, 2006: 56, 6.19). What understandings of human failure and pride, sin and salvation and redemption undergird the ambitions of urban regeneration? What, amidst the rhetoric of regeneration and renewal, are the agents of transformation choosing to elevate as their ultimate objects of worship?

In Sandercock's words, we see how the good city rests on the criteria of a well-balanced economy, altruistic citizenship, concern for social justice, environmental sustainability and inclusiveness, all grounded in a celebration of the promise of our shared humanity:

> The human spirit at the heart of planning engages every day in a dance of faith and hope, engages in a struggle to moderate greed with generosity, to conjoin private ambition with civic ambition, to care for others as much as or more than we care about ourselves, to think as much or more about future generations as we do about our own, to thoughtfully weigh the importance of memory alongside the need for

change, to greet a newcomer in the street rather than ignoring her, or worse, insulting him, or telling them to go back to where they came from. (Sandercock, 2006: 66)

The 'good city' or the 'human city'?

Other reports subsequently have attempted a similar taxonomy. The 'Human City Initiative', originating at the University of Birmingham, seeks to excavate the underlying values in our relationship to the city:

> What is our vision, as its creators, of the city in which we live or work? How does our experience shape what we see as possible and worthwhile for the life of the city? What does it mean to share a place with people who represent many different parts of the world? As citizens, for whom and what are we responsible? What powers govern our common life? Above all, what makes a city human? And how do we confront and root out what makes a city inhuman? (D. Clark, 2007: 3)

This report is critical of *Faithful Cities*' use of the terminology of the '*good* city', arguing that it is something only defined in relation to other qualities. This, we would argue, is the whole point! 'The good city' is a 'thick description' that contains many different criteria, which are interlocking and mutually dependent. The notion of 'goodness', however, is intended not only to embrace a sense of that which is pleasing, but also to connect with a long-established tradition of moral philosophy, of virtue ethics, in which the notion of the good is linked with understandings of human destiny and flourishing (Harris, 2006). A drawback to the terminology 'human' is that it neglects our connections to the well-being of the non-human, such as the environment; or that it misses the significance of the non-material, transcendent or spiritual which features even in human-ist writers such as Sandercock. The 'good city' not only meets our human, material needs but points us towards a greater good that necessarily transcends human self-interest.

The UN Habitat report for 2008–09 speaks of the 'harmonious city', a term which is also intended to hold together a number of related criteria of well-being and success. The concept of 'harmony' is chosen to express a necessary balance between the built and 'natural' environments, and between the objectives of social equity and ecological sustainability. While material measures are important tools of analysis, UN Habitat also points towards the significance of less tangible considerations. Note once more the affinities between these sentiments and earlier definitions, through even to the use of the terminology of 'soul' or spirit:

> This report adopts the concept of Harmonious Cities as a theoretical framework in order to understand today's urban world, and also as an operational tool to confront the most important challenges facing urban areas and their development processes. It recognises that tolerance, fairness, social justice and good governance, all of which are inter-related, are as important to sustainable urban development as physical planning ... The report also assesses the various intangible assets within cities that contribute to harmony, such as cultural heritage, sense of place and memory and the complex sets of social and symbolic relationships that give cities meaning. It argues that these intangible assets represent the 'soul of the city' and are as important for harmonious urban developments as tangible assets. (UN-Habitat, 2008: x)

Faithful capital

'Faithful capital' is a central concept of *Faithful Cities*, as a means of elaborating on the contribution that can be made by faith-based organisations to the enhancement of social networks which contribute to a healthy civil society. The discussion of faithful capital derives from Robert Putnam's work on 'social capital' as an index of the quality of people's ability to connect and work together towards common objectives via the processes that strengthen social bonds, transactions and institutions (Putnam, 2000; Field, 2003). Putnam describes it as 'connections among individuals – social networks and the norms of reciprocity and trustworthiness that arise from them' (Putnam, 2000: 19). Through these connections, which are further defined as 'bonding' (close-knit relationships based on family, ethnicity or class), 'bridging' (outward-looking relationships between diverse groups) and 'linking' (relationships which connect people to networks outside their normal peer groups), Putnam believes people are enriched and develop the skills and virtues necessary to build healthy civil society.

This, as the report itself claims, is the 'big idea' used to interpret much of the findings presented. In offering the wider community the outworkings of its vocabulary of 'love', 'hope', 'judgement', 'forgiveness', 'remembrance' and 'hospitality', Christian communities provide society with an alternative version of the urban narrative of regeneration and success to the account given by secular agencies (CULF, 2006: 3, 1.17). The implication is that it causes faith-based organisations to operate in a distinctive way, with a 'people-centredness', which is often at odds with the economically driven goals and working styles of commercial and statutory organisations with whom they might enter into fruitful, but critical, partnerships.

Similarly, 'faithful capital' can expand the civic vocabulary of conventional wisdom beyond the boundaries of tolerance (which can often mean indifference) to a more positive, if more costly, embracing of hospitality whereby 'strangers' are transformed into 'neighbours' and the foreigner, the asylum-seeker and the refugee, so often the objects of media vilification and popular suspicion, are regarded as honoured guests rather than alien threats (CULF, 2006: 23, 3.43). In an increasingly diverse society such resources of hospitality cannot be taken for granted and serve as vital antidotes to xenophobia and institutional racism (CULF, 2006: 21, 3.27). Furthermore, faithful capital is distinguished by practices that are rooted locally, and churches and other faith communities who have been involved in local neighbourhoods for many generations provide local communities with a collective sense of memory and rootedness in a particular place (CULF, 2006: 61, 6.39). It is by virtue of faithful capital that faith-based organisations play a vital role in regeneration, its 'major dividend' being people motivated to engage in their community by the conviction that 'other people and their circumstances matter' (CULF, 2006: 66, 7.2).

Faithful capital is thus an expression of what *Faithful Cities* terms a 'performative' theology. It means that faith, in terms of people's beliefs and actions, are indivisible in an essential unity of theology and practice. Theology is not mere abstract doctrine, or philosophical speculation, but a wellspring of stories, values and sensibilities that guide the life of faith. Yet that 'talk about God' is most authentic when it is practised, and not just preached: embodied in the faithful actions of worship, outreach and pastoral care. Theology is always practical because it is essentially about our words becoming flesh. For *Faithful Cities,* this serves to challenge the accusation that the church's involvement in social action or partnership is a distraction from its devotional practices. Rather, religious and spiritual practices are the disciplines that cultivate faithful capital that then 'pays dividends' in the shape of committed and transformative activism:

> The stories, scriptures, songs, prayers, rituals and teachings that form
> the everyday life of religious faith (the 'habits of the heart') are not
> some anthropological curiosity. They are the sources of the values
> which prompt action on behalf of those who are marginalized. The
> practices of faith and the actions on behalf of their neighbour cannot
> be separated. (CULF, 2006: 82, 8.22)

Part of the argument of *Faithful Cities*, however, was that the resources of
organised religion in many urban areas have gone unrecognised. This may
be partly due to government misunderstandings of the real nature of many
faith-based organisations – what is beginning to be called 'religious
literacy' (or lack of it) within the public and statutory sector. Some of this
may be due to the dominance of the secularisation thesis within the social
sciences, which means that the construction of racial and ethnic identities
(and their policy implications) has been discussed with little or no reference to, or comprehension of, religious affiliation (Smith, 2004:187).

Taking the long view

In May 2006, shortly before the launch of *Faithful Cities*, the Archbishop of
Canterbury introduced a debate in the House of Lords on the theme of
'Churches and Cities', largely anticipating the publication of this report.
What marked that debate was the way in which speaker after speaker rose
to affirm the value of the contribution of faith-based organisations: not
only in urban regeneration and community renewal, but in areas as diverse
as health-care chaplaincy, racial justice and social enterprise. *Faithful Cities*
also warned, however, against the way that the resources and the energy of
faith communities could be co-opted by the authorities or the capacities
and skills of local people undervalued in the process of regeneration. It
argues that faith is often misunderstood by policy-makers and those
steering regeneration projects; it argues for a grass-roots approach to
decision-making and community participation that places values of human
flourishing and a rounded sense of what makes a good city, as opposed to
narrowly economic criteria, as well as models of wealth creation that pay
attention to matters of equity and fair distribution.

For example, the reserves of 'faithful capital' are practically and tangibly
put to work in generating practical outcomes. But that also represents an
independent and critical voice that cannot simply be co-opted by expedi-

ency or sectional interest, since it should derive from independent values from the tradition of faith. While *Faithful Cities* endorses the importance of a critical solidarity with other planning and regeneration agencies, it also stresses that it is one in which faith-based organisations also interpose alternative priorities, perhaps with a different time-frame and more holistic values.

As the Archbishop of Canterbury put it in the House of Lords debate, '[Communities of faith] speak of a commitment and availability of social capital that is not likely to be withdrawn when things get difficult. In a world of time-limited grants and often desperate scrambling to create leadership and management structures that will survive the somewhat breathless rhythms of funding regimes, they allow a longer view' (R. Williams, 2006a). So religious congregations are places where the skills and capacities for social renewal are nurtured; and *Faithful Cities* calls on local and national government to acknowledge that faith-based organisations are well placed to help our urban neighbourhoods to flourish, materially and spiritually.

In a recent article, Andrew Davey points to the contradiction that faithful capital seems to concede precisely to the 'outcome-required' thinking that is supposedly anathema to faith-based organisations. He expresses discomfort with such a descent into functionalism, or the attempt to prove the 'usefulness' of religious groups. Davey argues that making the practice of faith a 'quantifiable product or commodity to attract attention or additional resources' has its dangers, and questions the use of the economic term 'capital', seeing little theological precedent for what he regards as moving beyond metaphor to reify 'the resources and assets of faith' (Davey, 2007: 16). Current interest in the capacity of faith-based organisations to deliver government policy and to be an agent of the less tangible values of social cohesion is thus open to criticism.

Similarly, the true capacity of faith-based organisations to deliver services when they themselves are fragile or in terminal decline is also clearly a stringent test of the long-term viability of the language of faithful capital. Greg Smith challenges the assumption that

> 'faith communities' have a large army of 'community leaders' poised to give their time to support the government's projects ... [which] seems wedded to a traditional Anglican concept of the role of the church, where a vicar with time on his/her hands is happy to work

un-controversially for the welfare of the whole community. However, the reality of religious life in the inner city is more likely to be one of over-stretched clergy, groups relying on lay (and socially excluded) leadership, faith that makes priorities of spiritual rather than social agendas, and sectarian or communal competition for scarce resources. (Smith, 2004: 195)

The issues of how the urban church maintains its service and engagement to the community without becoming captive to externally driven expectations is a topic to which we return in Chapter 8.

But what of the insistence in *Faithful Cities* on an inductive, contextual approach to doing theology, and an emphasis on the orthopraxy, rather than orthodoxy, of the urban church? Once more, we return to the tension between a praxis grounded in a tradition of 'common wisdom' and a church that regards an explicit call to faith expressed in the distinctiveness of the Gospel. It places debate about faithful capital within the ongoing debate surrounding 'service versus proclamation', social action versus evangelism, in the ministry of the church (Leech, 2006: 15). For Stephen Cox, the theological issue raised by faithful capital is the extent to which its core convictions about the nature of God and what it means to be human are truly shared by all faith traditions, as *Faithful Cities* claims, when for Christians, the revelation of God in Christ is unique to their understanding. How is the spiritual dimension of faithful action sustained if, in the partnership, people cannot pray together or 'make an explanation of the faith that motivates us … if we are not in agreement about that faith' (Cox, 2006: 4)? This raises questions, especially in partnership working, which is central to faithful capital, about how faithful capital can be built, sustained and given account of, when people involved in the same project come from different faiths and none. We may see this as an example of the tension we identified in Chapter 1 of this book: is the church an 'alternative performance' (CULF, 2006: 49, 5.21) whose own life of worship and distinctive, perhaps counter-cultural, witness constitutes its presence and identity; or is it called to enter into partnerships with others at the risk of diluting the Gospel? CULF opts for the performative praxis of seeing the face of Christ in the stranger and the needy (Matthew 25). A concern for the integrity of the church is not to take precedence over an affirmation of our common humanity under God; but it is nevertheless necessary to nurture the resources of faith, which serve as the wellsprings of activism.

Indeed, in a plural society Christians have to be prepared to give an account of themselves – and to find their faith deepened rather than diluted in the process:

> To withdraw behind the walls of places of worship, speaking only to one another, is to ignore the divine claim on the whole of creation and the divine invitation to become partners in the redemption of the world. But, if the Church is not to be compromised by partnerships, it must stay true to the core beliefs of its Christian vision. If it is, to use a metaphor of the prophet Isaiah (54.2) to 'lengthen its ropes' through partnerships with others, then it must also 'strengthen its pegs' by attention to worship, which touches the heart as well as the mind. (CULF, 2006: 75, 7.63)

Nevertheless, we should not dismiss questions of mission, evangelism and congregational growth. The urban church is trying to survive in a context of church decline; as Greg Smith's comments suggest, local congregations cannot afford to 'punch above their weight' indefinitely in terms of their commitments to their local neighbourhoods. This is a serious institutional question about the very long-term viability of the urban church itself and explains why some critics of *Faithful Cities* were disappointed on strategic as well as theological grounds with its failure to address the question of mission in an explicitly evangelistic sense. In its membership and in its theology, CULF did not take sufficient account of the emerging evangelical traditions who have moved into cities in the twenty years since *Faith in the City* and who combine practical projects with distinctive Christian witness: groups such as Eden, Faithworks and Urban Presence, as well as the growing prominence of Black-majority church traditions, both African and African-Caribbean.[4] Many of these groups combine a commitment to personal renewal as well as community transformation and have no difficulty in combining personal evangelical commitment with a call to social justice; they are also, statistically, among the fastest-growing constituencies of the urban church (Cox, 2006: 4).

Faithful Cities and beyond

> In this report, we argue that despite its ambivalent history, and its capacity to incite hatred and conflict, religious faith is still one of the

richest, most enduring and most dynamic sources of energy and hope for cities. Faith is a vital – and often essential – resource in the building of relationships and communities. In the values they promote, in the service they inspire, and in the resources they command, faith-based organisations make a decisive contribution to their communities. (CULF, 2006: 4, 1.28)

Of course, *Faithful Cities* was never likely to make the same kind of impact as *Faith in the City*. To its credit, *Faithful Cities*, following the lead of the Urban Bishops' Panel, acknowledged from the start that it was working in a more complex and less polarised context than its predecessor, and that its task was much more to comment on 'work in progress' than to issue indictments of government. So its core assumptions were, first, that government (central and local) could no longer be indicted with the same degree of neglect of urban priority areas as had been painfully evident to ACUPA; and second, that as a commission wishing still to address itself to both church and nation, it could nevertheless no longer guarantee a ready reception or the self-evidence of its findings, but would need to explain and make explicit the values and principles on which it took its stance. While these considerations may have muted the impact of *Faithful Cities*, they became the basis of some of its most important themes and conclusions: the notable improvements in the economic, cultural and physical state of many major English cities, and yet the continuing failure of 'trickle-down' policies of regeneration; the problematic, yet crucial, role of faith-based organisations and activity in many of our most marginalised urban areas; and the importance of bringing a values-based critique into an often fragmented and frenetic arena of policy initiatives, which can retain a larger picture and hold to a long-term view of developments.

Our reflection as members of the Commission is that it tried to draw together a wide variety of people with a range of different perspectives and starting points, and asked them to engage with a far more confused context than their predecessors on ACUPA twenty years earlier. Given the changing context, and the more equivocal evidence concerning government policy, it was perhaps inevitable that *Faithful Cities* was not as controversial or plain-speaking as *Faith in the City*. Nevertheless, the attempt was made to bridge the gap of the intervening two decades, to note the changes that called for new ways of working and thinking as well as insisting on significant continuities, such as the gap between rich and poor and the value of the churches' local presence and response.

One of the big contrasts between *Faith in the City* and *Faithful Cities* was that the former was about issues of justice that could be measured economically, in terms of poverty, environmental degradation and fiscal policy. It was a report, essentially, that emphasised material well-being. But even over the past five years it has become clear that the happiness and well-being agenda has to be addressed, something *Faithful Cities* managed to anticipate. And of course, this moves us into theological territory, because it touches on how people are valued, how we have freedom or not to participate and determine our futures, the way in which we discover, appreciate and inhabit the environment around us. For all its faults, then, *Faithful Cities* was successful in reflecting the changing times for the urban church, in the way it engages with public policy and in the way it does its theology; and it set in train a number of significant legacies.

First, two areas to which *Faithful Cities* gave insufficient attention were those of housing and education. While CULF was exercised by the proliferation of 'gated communities' of the relatively affluent in regenerated cities, it did not give enough space to the perspective of those in poor-quality accommodation or stranded on marginalised estates. In Chapter 4, we turn to those experiences and argue for alternative housing policies. In many respects, social class, in terms of determining opportunities, job prospects, educational attainment, is at the root of such segregation, greatly exacerbated by inflexibility in the housing market; but class remains the 'elephant in the room' in much regeneration policy.

Second, an emphasis within *Faithful Cities* on the diverse, complex but often intangible measures of a good or sustainable city remains a powerful heuristic tool. CULF speaks of 'five pillars of regeneration' – echoing the five great pillars of Islamic belief and practice – and the need to incorporate economics, governance, culture, environment and spirituality or meaning of life into our 'thick descriptions' of well-being. Third, *Faithful Cities* resulted in the appointment of Stephen Lowe as Bishop for Urban Life and Faith: the first Church of England bishop to have a permanent portfolio that was more than simply a specialist brief for House of Lords debates, but which has taken him the length and breadth of England on a journey of investigation and advocacy. It has also brought him into interaction with government at many different levels and enabled him to stimulate the very kind of debate around the 'good city' of which *Faithful Cities* dreamed.

This has had bearing on our understanding of the nature of public theology. If we are to ask, on what authority does the church speak out in public affairs, then one answer, possibly that of traditionalists, would be that bishops have authority from tradition and the historic form of church which is not subject to secular reason or public conventions. However, such a brief as that held by Stephen points towards another model of public intervention, with an authority to 'speak out' which comes from evidence-based argument, exposed to public view and derived from listening and attending to local voices and experiences. Indeed, the effectiveness of a figure such as a Bishop for Urban Life and Faith depends above all on his capacity to connect with such local activity and ensure that the concerns and realities of urban life and faith are projected onto a national stage. The chapters that follow are an attempt to continue that process of dissemination.

3
A Theology of Space and Place

Introduction

We have been emphasising throughout how one of the cardinal virtues of the urban church is its local nature. In the Anglican tradition, that is enshrined in the parish system, which guarantees that every square centimetre of the country falls under the responsibility of a local congregation. This is often expressed in terms of a parish priest holding the 'cure of souls' for the entire population in that place. In some ways, this may be seen as an odd anachronistic throw-back to the days of Christendom, even an uncomfortable vestige of Establishment arrogance; but as we shall explore in this chapter, such territorial jurisdiction, however that may be formally constituted in legal terms, does indeed keep alive an understanding of the whole of the created order in a particular area as belonging to God, and of a desire to render holy the local, the concrete and the particular as the specific context in which the church, as the spirit-filled Body of Christ, can help to further God's mission in that place. As the theologian Sigurd Bergmann has argued, it is about 'God taking place' (2008): a sacralisation of the physical, the spatial – and, as we shall argue, the environmental – as an arena of redemption. Bergmann also insists that the human desire to build and inhabit cities is a fundamentally *civilising* process – it is about forming 'culture' out of 'nature' – that accompanies the pragmatic desire for shelter and subsistence with a deep-rooted drive to mimic the creative nature of God. So 'God taking place' values the local and the spatial as an ephiphany of the divine, as a sacred space in which, through creative activity and the works of dwelling, humanity can experience something of the transcendent.

The 'spatial turn' in urban theory

The so-called 'spatial turn' (associated especially with the work of Edward Soja of UCLA) in urban geography, sociology and now urban theology reflects the contention that place is more than neutral, uninhabited space or a point on a map. Soja talks of 'writing the city spatially'. He asks, what does it mean to 'dwell together' in a particular space or place? Drawing on his intellectual mentor Henri Lefebvre, he says: 'all social relations remain abstract and unrealized until they are concretely expressed and materially and symbolically inscribed in lived space' (Soja, 2003: 275). 'Places' are thus never completely physical locations nor abstract concepts. Rather, places are spaces of social relations; they are constructed by human activity and human culture. 'A sense of place' requires people and societies to inhabit and occupy it and – crucially – to invest it with meaning. 'We don't live in an abstract framework of geometric spatial relationships, but in a world of meaning – existing in and surrounded by places, neither totally material or mental' (Cresswell, 1996: 13).

What is interesting about Soja's work is that it departs from classical Marxist social analysis, in which society evolves and develops via the passage of history and time – a perspective that Marx draws from Hegel – to an understanding of social relations and human community as essentially conducted, and constructed, in spatial rather than temporal terms. To think of society, and especially urban society, in this way transforms much of our perception; but in other respects, what Soja is saying is not new.

Cities of antiquity functioned around the creation of public space: citizenship was not conducted in an abstract or disembodied fashion, but in the midst of the marketplaces and civic forums which formed the basis for gathering, exchange and trade, debate and all major events. (Of course, the division between public and private space was also significant, and we should remember that some groups, notably women and slaves, were excluded from the public spaces and therefore from access to full citizenship.) In our survey of urban theory, we saw how the physical design of urban space itself was integral to the way in which planners, decision-makers and inhabitants conceived of their cities. In particular, modern urban theorists have stressed how the physical and spatial organisation of cities reflects deeper socio-economic dynamics. Engels' classic work on Manchester acutely observed the effects of spatial segregation which concentrated the urban poor into squalid dwellings in the city centre out of sight of the wealthy factory-owners and financiers who commuted in from the suburbs. Such segregation was a tangible, physical manifestation of what (for him) were the irrevocable polarities of class and power under industrial capitalism.

As we will argue in Chapter 4, a similar dynamic is being acted out in many of our contemporary council housing estates, where the isolation of many urban communities (especially white working class) continues the strong affinity between spatial segregation and social exclusion.

So attention to the ways in which we inhabit urban space and place as embodied beings, the ways in which urban planners, designers and policy-makers conceive the relationship between the organisation of urban space into public and private, affluent and deprived, is a very significant part of learning to 'read' the nature of our cities.

A walk through the city

Once we are conscious of the significance of space and place for under-standing some of the underlying dynamics of urban life, then we can become more conscious of how to shift from simply experiencing the givenness or 'everydayness' of inhabiting urban space, towards a more considered analysis of what it might mean. For some urban theorists and theologians, the device of narrating the personal impressions and experiences of simply walking through a city or neighbourhood has been a powerful and eloquent tool. Such writing draws out how space and place evoke – indeed are saturated in – rich associations of memory and meaning; and how the immediate, the specific and the concrete provide tangible and living examples of deeper values, stories and power relations that are perhaps less easy to realise in more abstract terms. As Philip Sheldrake argues, 'Physical places are vital sources of metaphors for social constructions of reality' (Sheldrake, 2000: 45).

The urban geographer Doreen Massey has written about returning to Wythenshawe, the 'garden city' public housing estate to the south of Manchester in which she grew up in the 1950s, and of her experience of walking through many of the familiar neighbourhoods of her youth (Massey, 2001). It is at one level a very personal and autobiographical account, yet she interweaves her own story with other stories as particular reminiscences send her into wider contexts: family history, the history of city planning in Manchester, issues of participation and governance, issues of urban theory. She uses the immediacy of her own experience to shape a wider, more analytical, approach; and yet it is, essentially, shaped by the physical sensation of walking and moving through space, as she encounters objects, buildings and artefacts that prompt deeper analysis. As Massey says, places '… are spaces of social relations' (Massey, 2001: 460), and '… the product of material practices' (Massey, 2001: 464) and she sets to work to expose the social, economic, symbolic transactions and relationships that have shaped those spaces and how people interact in them.

Massey highlights how the 'built environment' reflects deeper values and priorities: the changing nature of land and human settlements 'tell a story'. This is at the heart of Massey's narrative. She reflects on how the passage of people's lives is shaped by space and place, thus echoing Soja who is asking us to see that as a spatial, and not just an historical or temporal, phenomenon. Yet space and place – and the urban environment – are fundamentally embodied environments – 'those paving stones remind you of your frailty' (Massey, 2001: 471) – containing the narratives of individuals as well as entire communities.

In a similar vein, Barbara Glasson and John Bradbury, two Christian ministers in Liverpool, also illustrate this move from 'space' to 'place'. Walking around the city centre, they are doing more than moving through space; they are reflecting on how the 'lived experience' of the people of Liverpool is mediated through the stories that can be told about the changes that have occurred to landmark buildings and sites as a result of city-centre regeneration (Glasson and Bradbury, 2007).

Another set of juxtapositions is the local and the global – be it stories of migration or overseas holidaying. Today, Wythenshawe's position is increasingly dominated by Manchester Airport, with potential conflicts of interest. The physical proximity of these two places serves to illustrate a more general theme in urban theory: cities are quintessentially places of migration and movement, and magnets for new cultures and ideas. For Glasson and Bradbury, their walk to Liverpool's Pier Head vividly demonstrates this, and how a neutral 'space' is imbued with a sense of 'place'. The docks are a physical monument to the city's historical status as a great port, and yet they speak too of loss and dispossession, of Liverpool's economic decline, and of the untold stories of those for whom the Pier Head was either their first or last glimpse of the city:

> To the outsider it [Pier Head] is an empty expanse of land between the
> Liver buildings and the river estuary. But in the history of Liverpool it

is the emotive point of arrivals and departures that has marked the history of immigration and emigration; from the slave ships arriving with human, textile and sugar cargoes to the Cunarders setting sail on world tours, the Pier Head has been a place of new lives beginning. A place of abject poverty as the hungry fled the potato blights of Ireland and a place of riches as the ship owners dispatched their cargoes. *Our history is about migration. Diaspora in, and out again. The city is an organic thing.* We meet the conjunctions of people, place and story – and the Pier Head embodies something particular only to Liverpool's people, place and story. (Glasson and Bradbury, 2007: 28; our emphasis)

Glasson and Bradbury also stress the dynamic movement of the city. While they stress the power of memory to grant a particular meaning to physical space, and recognise that change can bring the loss of things of value, they also bring to our attention the essence of a city in its ever-changing qualities as a living, growing entity. This, along with the inescapability of global diversity – which, as Glasson and Bradbury rightly identify, has been a part of Liverpool's story since the beginning – will form part of our themes in Chapter 5.

Massey also links the history of the building and settlement of a particular place, Wythenshawe, with wider economic and cultural history: in her case, a particular era of British social policy after 1945, and of 'old Labour' public expenditure and central planning. Today, patterns of 'governance' and participation are different – residents are not tenants of a council landlord but stakeholders, clients or 'partners' in local authority regeneration schemes. The housing stock, and the way in which the physical fabric of the houses has been improved by owner-occupiers, tells that story in a visual and graphic fashion.

However, as Massey comments, ' "Public space" turns out to be a tricky concept' (2001: 471), as contested space exposes something of the dynamics of power. Just as different groups' inhabitation of space can work along segregated lines, so too questions of access and exclusion reveal something of a community's fault-lines of normalisation and deviance. For Glasson and Bradbury, this is illustrated by the flow of pedestrians around Paradise Street, a flagship new city-centre retailing and leisure complex. The redesigning of urban space has meant that some older shops have been squeezed out and security guards discourage 'undesirables' such as skateboarders or homeless people from gathering. This leads them to ask critical questions about public access and ownership of space, and how urban spaces are occupied, owned, colonised, neglected and even subverted. For them, the restrictions placed on public access around such developments represent the triumph of corporate business, and the hegemony of the global brand, a universal language, over a diversity of 'vernacular' cultures: 'What is the "narrative" that forms "culture"? Is it a dominant story of success at the expense of the silenced ...? ... Whose Babel is this? Whose place is this? Whose story is this? The global and the multinational tell the story, own the place and determine which people will be in it' (Glasson and Bradbury, 2007: 31–2).

The ways in which urban space is controlled and managed is, once more, an embodiment of deeper dynamics of economic, cultural, social and political exclusion. Massey's memories of Wythenshawe and Glasson and Bradbury's observations on Liverpool give some indication of how the topography of urban design and built environment make statements about corporate identity and civic pride (the idea of a city), what it means to be human/a citizen/a consumer (and whose vision is this), and even how the self-conscious use of 'monumental space' (Massey 2001: 472), especially in the context of urban regeneration, sets up secular objects of ultimate aspiration and worship (Glasson and Bradbury, 2007: 31).

Essentially, what all three authors are doing might be termed 'autoethnography': auto meaning self (as in auto-biography) and ethnography meaning writing about culture or people, a familiar method within disciplines such as anthropology and sociology, where a researcher will engage with a different culture to their own as 'participant observer'. In 'writing the city' through the personal experience of moving through its urban spaces, Massey, Glasson and Bradbury are 'turning life into text' and demonstrating that spaces are bearers of narratives, symbols and memories. Philip Sheldrake also uses this image: 'It is therefore appropriate to think of places as texts, layered with meanings' (Sheldrake, 2000: 54).

All this represents a valuing of material culture and the built environment to speak of more than mere subsistence – and indeed to be more than empty 'space' – but to be capable of evoking and embodying deeper meanings and associations. It is testimony to our ability as human beings to shift seamlessly between the physical and the metaphysical; and how intangible things like meaning, memory, loss, power, love and loyalty are deeply embedded in a physical context. As some theologians have argued, this is one way in which we can think of humanity as made in the image of

God: of inhabiting material culture, yet capable of transcending mere physicality and matter (without abandoning or negating it) in an expression of our striving towards God (Hefner, 2003; Graham, 2002). It is a reminder of the juxtaposition of the immanent and the transcendent in our cities.

The 'sustainable city': environmental and ecological perspectives

How we inhabit physical space and transform it into 'place' is thus an evocative theme, and provides another example of how urban theory and theology can converge. But there is another fundamental sense in which cities are also dependent on their material environment for their survival and well-being, namely their physical sustainability. Increasingly, not only within the great industrial or post-industrial cities of the West, but in the emerging mega-cities of the global South, the question of cities not just as civic centres of governance, financial hubs or centres of population and culture, but as organic systems which are dependent on land and other 'natural' resources, exposes yet further, increasingly urgent, dimensions of the physicality and spatial effects of urban life – and of what affects 'the good city'.

The United Nations Human Habitat report of 2008–09 took as its theme the 'Harmonious City', which is interpreted not only in terms of harmony between different human interest groups and communities, but also between the built and 'natural' environments. As we have seen, the UN's concept of the harmonious city comprises many of the qualities echoed elsewhere as the marks of a good or human city; but increasingly, questions of economic equity, fair governance and cultural vitality are complemented by a growing urgency to ensure environmental well-being.

This is about the impact of urbanisation on the natural habitat and the impact of urban growth on the surrounding region. Urbanisation presents serious problems of environmental pollution, congestion, deforestation, global warming, depletion of non-renewable energy sources, extinction of species, population growth and pollution. The rise of environmental and green politics represents one response to these realities. They encourage urban dwellers to live within their means, reduce environmental impact and consider the global nature and impact of urban living. Yet ultimately they invite us to consider all cities as vitally dependent on their surrounding environment and to see the spatiality of the city in *ecological* terms – as a vast, interlocking, interdependent system. To put things in such a perspective inevitably demands that we consider whether the urban spaces and places we build are sustainable in terms of their relationship to and dependence on the planet itself: to ask, what kind of place would the sustainable city be? How would it feel to inhabit it? How would it need to be designed and managed; what is its materiality; how must it 'take place'?

The 1970s saw the emergence of environmental awareness and a new environmental movement. An early, seminal text was Rachel Carson's *Silent Spring* (1962), which argued that use of pesticides and synthetic chemicals was having a disastrous effect on wildlife. *Limits to Growth* (Meadows, 2005 [1972]) painted a somewhat apocalyptic picture of the impact of population growth and consumer consumption on the earth's resources, predicting economic collapse by the beginning of the twenty-first century. The United Nations sponsored a number of influential initiatives on the environment, beginning with the Conference on the Human Environment in Stockholm (1972), bringing issues such as depletion of the ozone layer to public attention. The report, 'Our Common Future', often referred to as the Brundtland Report, emerged out of the 1987 World Commission on Environment and Development and argued that future patterns of world economic development must make environmental sustainability a priority. It was followed by the 1992 Earth Summit and the 'Rio Declaration', which attempted to establish global agreements in areas such as sustainable development, environmental dumping, pollution and use of fossil fuels. Programmes such as the United Nations Human Settlements Programme (UN-HABITAT) and the Commission on Sustainable Development continue to promote research, consultation and legislation on sustainability.

The Brundtland Report defined the sustainable city as 'development that meets the needs of the present without compromising the ability of future generations to meet their own needs' (World Commission on Environment and Development, 1987: 8), although we might ask what factors – economic, cultural, political – determine our needs? The World Conservation Union described sustainable development in 1991 as 'improving the quality of human life while living within the carrying capacity of supporting ecosystems' (Wheeler, 1996: 489). Also around this time, the architect Richard Rogers delivered the prestigious Reith Lectures for the BBC (1995), which were entitled 'Cities for a Small Planet', subsequently published under the same name (Rogers, 1997). He argues that the sustainable city is:

- A Just City, expressing social and economic equity; where justice, food, shelter, education, health care and other social goods are fairly distributed, and where people have freedom to determine their own futures, through fair and democratic governance.
- A Beautiful City, where the built environment has the capacity to stir the soul and move the spirit – where we are nourished and sustained aesthetically as well as materially.
- A Creative City, where people are given scope to extend their potential, to be open-minded and innovative.
- An Ecological City, which minimises its environmental impact, with a balance between landscape and built environment and where buildings and infrastructure are resource-efficient and not exhausting basic stock of reserves of ecological capital .
- A City of Easy Contact, with accessible public space which encourages social mixing, fosters community and mobility and invites contact and communication, both interpersonal and electronic.
- A Compact and Polycentric City, which protects the countryside, integrates neighbourhoods and maximises proximity of communities.
- A Diverse City, where difference is valued and public life is premised on new ideas and dynamic communities. (Rogers, 1997: 167–8).

Yet as the title of the Rogers' lectures and book suggest, these criteria are to be measured not just in terms of general goodness, well-being or quality of life: the good city is all these things, but it must increasingly be organised around a recognition of its responsibility to *future* as well as current generations, its interdependence on wider natural habitat and the limits to growth.

Sustainable development is therefore 'development that improves the long-term health of human and ecological systems' (Wheeler, 1996: 487), with a stress on long-term solutions, inter-disciplinary, multi-agency planning. According to Wheeler, its chief principles are as follows:

- Compact, efficient land use. Restrictions on urban sprawl, regulations on land use and building. Move away from land as property; connection between human land use and nature.

- Less automobile use, public transport.
- Efficiency in use of resources, less pollution and waste; renewables.
- Restoration of natural systems – e.g. canals and wildlife, allotments, urban farms.
- Good, affordable housing with access to facilities, open spaces, transport, mixed communities.
- A healthy 'social ecology' – social justice, anti-discrimination, capacity-building, opportunity.
- Sustainable economics – developing economic system and decisions that value long-term health and sustainability.
- Community participation and democracy – in planning, decision-making, etc.
- Preservation of local cultures and knowledges, not least to value local uniqueness. (Wheeler, 1996)

It is interesting to note how far these are about not just how a city organises its fundamental activities, but also crucially how it utilises physical space in the process. Environmental concerns are therefore inextricably linked with issues of material resources, with 'space' as one of those factors to be deployed strategically, including a city's infrastructure and internal design, in order to minimise (spatial) congestion and lessen the carbon footprint, to encourage use of renewable energy, reduce pollution and overcrowding.

Yet predominantly, sustainability involves living within one's means – almost a concept of ecological capital, which is not exhausting basic stock of resources and not drawing on reserves. It reflects also, perhaps, a shift away from modernist metaphors of the city as 'machine' towards more organic, ecological models, of a city that is a living entity, which is adaptable, capable of evolving, a dynamic organic phenomenon, delicately balanced and interdependent with its surroundings. To adopt a Darwinian perspective, therefore, the 'good city' is one capable of maximising its fitness to maintain long-term adaptability and responsiveness to change in order to survive and prosper.

Tim Beatley, a leading proponent of what is termed 'green urbanism', argues that increasingly the design of cities must be modelled on naturalistic rather than machine-like analogies, overcoming earlier preferences for artificial and mass-produced surroundings in favour of an alternative, more symbiotic relationship between urban centres and their surrounding environments. Can cities be like forests (William McDonough) – fresh air and water; restorative, invigorating, productive, green?

Tim Beatley also argues that cities need to adopt a circular rather than linear metabolism, with a symbiotic relationship with the environment – wasting nothing, recycling, extracting resources from waste; with greater connection between inputs and outputs. They need to move towards greater self-sufficiency, with greater awareness of their dependency on local, regional and global hinterlands, for example with regard to food miles. Beatley argues that the physical topography of cities must contribute to the facilitation of more sustainable, healthy lifestyles, with connections to nature as essential to well-being, and which give people opportunities for a good range of choices using sustainable methods, such as affordable, convenient and varied forms of transport. Finally, Beatley's green urbanism advocates a principle we have already encountered, that of more mixed communities, and the creation of sustainable neighbourhoods, which are attractive to live in, self-sufficient, and which meet the needs of local people. Thus we can see how the 'ecology' of a city – its functioning as an interdependent, sufficient system – leads us back to the debate about the good city, but reminds us that all criteria for the well-being of an urban community have to be held in balance, each contributing to the others.

Commentators are swift to insist, however, that this is more than simply introducing some provision for recycling of waste; it actually represents the 'greening' of all aspects of a city's life. If *ecology* is about the essential interconnectedness of all things, then that is certainly reflected in green urbanism and concerns for environmental sustainability, since the viability of cities in environmental terms is seen as holistic, a question of the *interdependence* of a range of indices of well-being. The emergence of environmental movements has offered further impetus to think about challenges to sustainability and to rethink doctrines of progress and economic growth as inevitable (perhaps, even underpinned by a Hegelian view of history), towards a different paradigm where space and place and our embodied interdependence as part of a global organism becomes the predominant paradigm.

From the 'secular' to the 'sacred' City

In this section, we want to explore further what it would mean for urban theology to undertake its own 'spatial turn'; away from a privileging of salvation history, of God acting within human temporal experience, towards an idea of God 'taking place' (Bergmann, 2007). How would such a spatial turn shape a theological reading of the sustainable city; and what would it mean for the future priorities of the urban church – how it 'takes place' or takes shape in sacred space.

Sigurd Bergmann identifies two main directions in which theology might recover an understanding of space and place and in the process develop a deeper ecological and environmental sensibility. Essentially, it is about making, and apprehending, the physical environment as sacred. First, he considers how classic questions and themes from the Bible and Christian doctrine might be recast in the light of the turn to spatiality. He argues that this enables an enrichment of many images and practices that have been marginalised, especially within the Western traditions. As he argues, 'religion ... does not work at all without or beyond space' (Bergmann, 2008: 71). He wants to reappropriate space as the dominant metaphor through which God is revealed to humanity and through which humanity encounters transcendence. 'Even processes of building and urban planning can be studied by theologians as religious phenomena and expressions of experiences with God' (Bergmann, 2008: 72). This reflects Bergmann's earlier work on contextual theology – talk about God is always shaped by the world and culture in which it comes to speech.

'In accordance with biblical and classical theology, space could and should be regarded as the Creator's gift to the living, and place as the foundational dimension of reflecting on the Son's incarnation and the Spirit's inhabitation on earth' (Bergmann, 2007: 2). This entails a theology of creation; of affirming material, embodied experience; and a theology of the Holy Spirit as infusing and animating the built environment to make a place 'sacred'.

'Urbanisation as a religious process'

Bergmann also advances the idea that the very process of urbanisation may be seen as a kind of religious quest or practice. Human beings are not simply content to build dwellings that offer physical shelter and security; their needs transcend material survival, with a deep instinct to settle in places that seem especially sacred or meaningful, and through the reshaping of a natural landscape, create a habitat that for its makers symbolises deeper relationships to nature, the divine and one another. Despite a tendency to deal in archetypes, Bergmann reiterates our recurrent thread of a strong link between the material and spiritual dimensions of human culture: 'The city knits the divine life-giving powers of the subterranean world to the formation, development and history of the people between water, earth and heaven' (Bergmann, 2008: 75).

'How to make oneself at home'

Bergmann also adopts the idea of 'home' (in German, *Heimat*) as a significant theological theme, and obviously this is related to the spatial turn as well. Technology has given us the illusion of no longer being dependent on the 'natural' environment, and cloaked our awareness of the vital links between urbanisation and the wider ecology of relationships, both natural and social. At least, says Bergmann, climate change is serving to alert us to our vulnerability and our basic dependence on the earth's long-term sustainability for our very survival! But urbanisation brings with it an alienation from these realities: 'Houses are [no] longer built by their inhabitants; cities are not any longer planned and constructed by their communities; even battles are not fought face to face, but rather are electronically mediated and technically purified in so-called "clean" military strikes' (Bergmann, 2008: 79).

But the instinct to 'make oneself at home' endures. Even if it is a cardboard box in a shanty town, the human desire to 'indwell' a space, to create a habitat, to exercise creative agency in transforming our environment is unquenchable. Yet for the theologian, it says something profound about what it means to be human, and what it says about the nature of God. 'What kind of a god, or belief in the ultimate, works at the heart of such constructions?', asks Bergmann (2008: 79–80). Architecture and planning have a physical shape or design, but they are also embodiments of ideological constructions of the perfect city. What would it mean, asks Bergmann, if human settlements were to organise the business of making themselves at home around 'a fourfold love': of environment, neighbour, God and oneself – which Bergmann characterises as the quintessential Judao-Christian ethic? This, for him, is akin to the 'good city'; but it is fundamentally about allowing the spirit of God to infuse and transform the very human impulse of building and dwelling: 'what does it mean that the God of the Here and Now acts and liberates in urban space? More briefly put: how and where does God take place, and what happens? Where does the Holy Spirit *make herself at home*?' (Bergmann, 2008: 82, our emphasis).

'Beyond amnesia'

Bergmann continues this theme of whether cities alienate us from the ecology of life, or whether they are capable of connecting us with a divine impulse, by using the motifs of forgetting and remembering. He thus picks up the theme of 'memory', which as we have seen is recurrent within contemporary urban theory (Sandercock) and theology.

> Does the city have a memory? How does urban space destroy or enhance the depth of the citizens' memory? ... How could remembrance of the past and the sufferings of foregoing generations be expressed spatially ...? Should Christian religion in this context mainly function as an advocate for the city's unity and its long-term memory, and is biblical religion in this context a plea to work with the city's memory? (Bergmann, 2008: 85–7)

In his book *Spaces for the Sacred* (2000), Philip Sheldrake reflects on the frequently cited forecast that by 2025 over two-thirds of the world's population will be city-dwellers. For Sheldrake, however, this is more than a question of demographics or even environmental and ecological concern: it is a *theological* question about the meaning and purpose of cities: what role do they play in our understanding of what it means to be truly human, truly alive?

> The city is where, for an increasing proportion of humanity, 'the practice of everyday life' takes place, either constructively or destructively. The growth rate of cities urgently requires that we give attention not merely to design and planning but also to deeper questions of meaning and purpose ... The challenge is how to relate city-making to a vision of the human spirit and what enhances it. (2000: 1)

Note once more the juxtaposition of what we termed the *material* and the *metaphysical*: human beings are creative animals, builders of worlds, but these worlds could be physical objects like cathedrals, canals or cafes, or worlds of meaning and imagination, like films, stories, religious symbolism, or myth. Often the two cannot be disentangled: consider the way films or novels capture hopes and fears about the future of the city. Consider also the way space and place embody different values and priorities, as in the work of Glasson and Bradbury and Massey, for example.

But Sheldrake takes the notion of the spatiality of cities and begins to develop an understanding of how the sense of cities as simultaneously human material constructions and sites of meaning might be transformed into a kind of social ethic for planners. He reflects on the relatedness of the two Latin words *urbs* (physical place, dwellings, buildings) and *civitas* (the collective of people gathered together) in our language for the urban, the city, citizenship, civil society. Cities are places *and* people. Similarly, urban planning is never just about material resources: someone, somewhere is making decisions based on their own view of the good city. Cities have their own history and no new projects ever start with a blank sheet.

Sheldrake is ambivalent about Christianity's anti-urban inheritance, and in particular how space and place might be considered 'sacred'. Are the cities of biblical literature cursed and godless places? Did Augustine prefer the spiritual realm of the city of God over that of the immediacy of the earthly city? Sheldrake argues that what matters theologically is the quality of the human community embodied in the city: 'what makes a city are people not walls' (2000: 14). The ideal of cathedral life expressed this in medieval times: all human life was there! The problem comes with secularization after the Enlightenment (eighteenth century) when ' "the sacred" retreated from public place and life ... into the purified spaces of religious buildings and into the private realm' (Sheldrake, 2000: 40).

Note once more this recurrent 'post-secular' theme of the late twentieth/early twenty-first centuries of restoring a lost apprehension of 'the sacred' back into public space. Sheldrake argues that there is a need to reclaim our sense of space and place, to repopulate them with narratives and to see them as the stage on which 'the practice of everyday life' (quoting de Certeau) takes place. So once more, Sheldrake adopts the prevailing 'spatial turn' but argues not simply for an understanding of 'place' as one of memory and meaning, but as 'sanctified' or sacred space:

> 'The sacred' is not removed from the world and history onto another plane ... The sacred is articulated in a variety of ways, of which spatial structures are one example ... 'The sacred' involves attending to what is more than immediate pragmatic concerns. In other words, it encapsulates a vision of ultimate value in human existence. (2000: 41)

The key rests in *particularity*, in recognising the importance of the material world, our physical surroundings, even the built environment, for reminding us of who we are and where we belong.

> The concept of 'place' refers not simply to geographical location but also to a dialectical relationship between environment and human narrative. 'Place' is any space that has the capacity to be remembered and to evoke what is most precious. It evokes a distinctive sense of the 'thisness' or particularity that lies at the heart of incarnational faith … It is for this reason that the human sense of place remains a critical theological and spiritual issue. (Sheldrake, 2000: 43)

We need to transform what Sheldrake terms 'non-place' (after the anthropologist Marc Augé) with a sense of 'place' that offers a renewed sense of identity and belonging. It is interesting to note how, once more, Sheldrake turns to ideas of narrative – of valuing the stories and experiences of the 'everyday' as the raw stuff of which our glimpses of the sacred and transcendent might emerge:

> Narrative is the key to our identity. We need stories to live by to make sense of otherwise unrelated life events and also to find a sense of dignity. It is only by enabling alternative stories to be heard that an elitist 'history' is prised open, offering access to the oppressed, to the people normally excluded from the history of public places. Without a narrative, a person's life is merely a random sequence of unrelated events: birth and death are inscrutable, temporality is a terror and a burden, and suffering and loss remain mute and unintelligible. (2000: 55)

Modernity stresses universalism and anonymity at the expense of specific and personal. But theologically, the incarnation enables a valuing of the specific (human lives, bodies, relationships and narratives) within the universal (God as source of all things). This calls forth respect for both our own particularity and also that of others as part of a shared community of human creatures. Note once more how Christian theology is understood as having a role to play as counter-narrative to the alienation of modernity by providing rituals, narratives and communities that link people both to their immediate world and to a common human story. The church can embody this in the Eucharist: celebration of material existence as vessel of redemptive grace, an act of particularity in a given time and place that links to a universal Christian practice. We will have more to say about the significance of church buildings in Chapter 8.

Cities have a role and purpose to play in improving people's lives. A new generation of urban planners such as Leonie Sandercock operate according to this very 'person-centred' understanding of urban development. For her, values of imagination, play, agency and spirituality – especially as embedded in particular places and spaces – lie at the heart of what makes a *humane* city. Our own personal experience of observing the use of space in cities like Chicago and Vancouver would endorse this sentiment. Both cities have resisted the privatisation of urban land – especially access to the waterfront – and promoted the use of such public spaces for leisure and exercise. Writing about Chicago's Millennium Park in our report for CULF in 2004, we noted the sense of play and freedom that such spaces inspired:

> The fountain attracted legions of children, many of whom seemed to have come prepared with their bathing suits to participate actively in the proceedings! It was a genuinely delightful area, full of a sense of play and fun which perfectly encapsulated the mood of the entire Park ... Indeed, one remarkable feature of Chicago is the amount of public, green, leisure space, both at the heart of the city off North Michigan Ave and down by the waterfront where there are numerous paths for cyclists, walkers and joggers, as well as many boat marinas on the lake. This is a hallmark of the Daley administration's management of land and development, although there is a strong populist and campaigning tradition around defending waterfront space and other communal areas from commercial encroachment. (Graham and Lowe, 2004: 11–12)

The 'conjunction of people, place and story' (Glasson and Bradbury, 2007: 28) that is associated with the so-called 'spatial turn' is first and foremost an embodied, sensual experience of space, as the sounds, sights – and smells! – of a place evoke deeper processes and dynamics. In a profound way, the 'material' reflects the 'metaphysical' or 'symbolic' and gives us access to ways in which people invest the built environment with memories, narratives and values. Yet the design of urban space, and how we live and move within it, tells other stories of power and exclusion, political and economic. And whether it is to be told in the secular 'temples' of retailing, or civic pride, or the indwelling of sacred space, there are stories to be told about who and what we worship, and what that symbolises about the shape of the good city.

4

A Nation Divided: The Challenge Facing our Cities

Divided by ... class

The journey from central London to South Oxhey, locked away in a corner of South Hertfordshire, is a parable of our nation's divisions. The Metropolitan Line runs fast to Moor Park; the more convenient station for South Oxhey is on a slow stopping service. Moor Park station is part of one of the more exclusive housing estates in England where the value of property is counted in millions not thousands. Drive your car through the estate and the surveillance cameras flash your registration to you on a smartly constructed display screen to remind you that your progress is being monitored through Moor Park. Once you have escaped, NATO's and Allied Command's vast facilities at Northwood with their high fences and air of mystery are the next point of interest until you turn left through the woods into the one road leading to South Oxhey.

South Oxhey is a large council housing estate built in the late 1940s and early 1950s to accommodate London overspill and victims of the Blitz. It sits in one of the most prosperous areas in the country and during the initial public enquiry in 1944 the surrounding local residents demanded that the estate must be invisible from any direction. It still is. It is surrounded by thick woods, which hide it and separate it from all its wealthy neighbours, a process which leads to low self-image and a feeling of stigmatisation by neighbouring communities. As the local vicar Pam Wise says, 'There is much material poverty but there is a much greater poverty of spirit.'

The population is about 12,000, of which 93% are white British, but in recent years there has been a steady growth in the number of ethnic minorities, mainly black Africans. BBC *Newsnight* in January 2004 reported on the high level of anti-social behaviour on the estate, which was particularly imbued with racism. Policing improved as a consequence of the bad publicity, but still, if the blogs on South Oxhey life are anything to go by, the problems have not gone away.

> 'CHAV (council house and violent) yeah I'd say that summed most of them up in South Oxhey. The younger chavs trying to uphold long gone past reputations of their dads, mums and uncles. All declaring they hate anyone who 'ain't white and british ...' ('beentheredunit', 2007)

> 'The area has a 50 year tradition of breeding a particularly nasty Chav strain, who really see little hope of anything in life, and this has bred into them a HATRED of anyone who has the faintest whiff of aspiration about their person.' ('supacreep', 2005)

South Oxhey's statistics are by no means extreme in national terms. There are low levels of skills among the working population, a high proportion of lone parents, a high proportion claiming benefits, and lower life expectancy than the surrounding areas. Educational achievement is low with only 15% of students leaving the nearest secondary school (not on the estate) achieving 5 GCSEs A–C including English and Maths – a truly appalling figure. In 2006 Hertfordshire County Council passed a motion that resulted in South Oxhey children no longer being eligible to attend the closest (and best) schools in Watford, but the priority catchment area became Borehamwood which is eleven miles away without any direct transport links – a journey would take about two hours. One of the local primary head teachers said that she has children arriving at school unable to speak and still in nappies.

The Church of All Saints South Oxhey started a project called ASCEND in 1996. Its main focus is on helping people improve their skills and gain access to work. One of the major problems has been the high number of learners whose literacy skills are below pre-entry level (reading ages of 5–6 years) and ASCEND has begun to work with this group. Hearing the story of adults in their 40s who had received the first certificate in their lives as they began to learn to read is extremely moving. In a year, 595 clients received training on their courses and 643 used their

Information, Guidance and Advice service. Since the service started, 550 have moved into paid or voluntary employment.

Yet the project's financial position has been precarious. Government funding disappeared and the round of grant applications has been a burden to the trustees who are largely drawn from neighbouring wealthier churches. Closure was held off by an emergency grant from the Church Urban Fund until a Big Lottery Fund application was successful, giving some security for the medium term. Even more exciting has been the selection of South Oxhey by the BBC as a focus for *The Choir*, a series where a conductor is encouraged to draw together people with no musical experience to sing publicly. Pam Wise put forward South Oxhey as a location and the programme worked with local schools and an adult choir for almost a year. Sixty seats were put out for the first adult meeting. Two hundred turned up and the newly formed choir was soon performing in Westminster Abbey and at an open-air concert for the community. The power of culture to promote community cohesion is something to which we return later.

There are areas with greater levels of deprivation than South Oxhey. It is exceptional because it forms a large pocket of deprivation in an area of great wealth. Three Rivers District Council is under no great pressure to focus resources into the area as its political complexion is not going to be materially affected by the votes from South Oxhey. There is no major regeneration programme still working in the area; Single Regeneraton Budget schemes have been and gone, leaving few marks of real progress. In so many ways it represents divided Britain, hidden from middle-class eyes other than television reality police documentaries, which convey the raw violence that a minority of disaffected young people visit on these communities.

South Wye, in the cathedral city of Hereford, is another large council estate in a different but still comparatively wealthy environment. Here the local Anglican church is involved in running a needle exchange as part of a community advice centre project in a neighbourhood shop. The housing stock is variable in quality and skills and employment levels on the estate are still low. Drug addiction is the highest level in the county and present serious problem to the health authority and police. There has been a Si Regeneration Programme on this estate and some effort is being m infill some of the vacant land with new owner-occupied housing, b is still a pervading sense of desolation which is all too easily to be these large council estates.

Benchill in Wythenshawe used to be the most deprived ward in the country. Manchester City Council and central government adopted a twin-track approach to this part of the overspill estate of 60,000 in the shadow of Manchester airport. First, developers were invited in to provide smart new housing behind high fences and walls at a subsidised cost, as land values were low. Second, the poorly maintained social housing was handed over to a newly formed housing trust, Willow Park. Managing 8,000 homes, it sees itself as transforming housing and improving the quality of life in Wythenshawe with a wide range of activities including training, security measures, debt advice and community development initiatives. The Audit Commission gave it a 3-star top rating and it has had a succession of awards for its work in the area.

Each of these three examples illustrates the dangers of monochrome social/council housing estates that are replicated in hundreds of similar stories from East Hull to Plymouth, and even in some of our smaller rural communities with the council housing separated off from the rest of the village community. These estates have become symbols of the class divisions in our society. The *Guardian* undertook a survey published on 20 October 2007, which shows that after ten years of Labour Government social change in Britain is almost static.

> The poorest people in society are most aware of the impact of the class system, with 55% of them saying that it is class not ability, that greatly affects they way they are seen ... Many class attitudes have survived economic change. That suggests people are still judged by where they come from rather than how much they earn.

Chelmsley Wood in Birmingham is a more modern edition of Wythenshawe in Manchester. Built in the late 1960s Chelmsley Wood was created with a view to providing everyone on Birmingham's long council house waiting list with a place to live. Lynsey Hanley tells a graphic and moving story of growing up on this new estate, mixing it with a review of much of the story of council housing since the war. She finishes her book with these words:

> 'The estate where I grew up', wrote a Birmingham Post reporter in 1971, 'is a town of strangers. [The] Wood, where there is a town itching to be born, but is prevented because they haven't delivered the

blood yet, the community spirit, and where the wind gathers in rude pockets around the corners of the precincts. (Why are these new straight square precincts always so windy?)'

> The empty town of strangers gave me space and light, but it didn't give me a chance to see what life could be like outside it. You cannot know what that was like unless you grew up inside it. Breaking out of it was like breaking out of prison. For all its careful planning and proximity to the city and the country, the estate was ringed by that invisible, impenetrable force field: the wall in the head. That may say as much for the closed ranks of the working class as it does for the failures of town planning. But I know that I will never scale another wall quite so high. (Hanley, 2007: 233–4)

A bishop living on a council estate is an unusual phenomenon. The challenge of living in by far the largest house in the area (an old vicarage) is no different from that facing many council estate clergy. 'How many bedrooms do you have in your house? 'Six'. 'Why' are there only two of you living in your house with six bedrooms and there are eight of us living in our three-bedroom house?' Little wonder there was an arson attack on the house that did serious damage to the downstairs. When 20 urban clergy working in demanding contexts were taken away for a 48-hour break it was the level of violence and vandalism that many of them experienced on their council estates that shocked one of the facilitators, the Rector of Moss Side. In an area that is synonymous with gun crime, she had never experienced the routine anti-social behaviour that was the pattern of life for many living on council estates.

In a project sponsored by the Joseph Rowntree Foundation, Rebecca Tunstall and Alice Coulter examined the improvements that have taken place as a result of various government regeneration initiatives between 1991 and 2001. They found that

> the socio–economic gaps between the estates and their local authorities and the nation identified in previous studies have been reduced, particularly in terms of unemployment rates, although all 20 estates still had higher levels of unemployment and economic activity than their local authorities and 19 had higher concentrations of children. Economic activity was an exception, increasing in the estates in

1991–2001 … The changes in the estates over the period 1980–2005 include, and were partly driven by, the fact that they have become more mixed in tenure and economic status. (Tunstall and Coulter 2006)

Social class: the elephant in the room?

There can be no doubt that successive interventions and investment by central government over the last twenty years has significantly improved the physical profile of many of our council estates. What is also clear from some of the stories coming from those areas is that there is still much to be done, particularly in the state of residents' well-being and happiness. Social and class mobility seems frozen. Educational achievement, despite enormous investment, seems slow to turn the corner while aspirations remain low. We would argue, however, that for our cities to experience real regeneration the narrowing of these gaps and greater integration of communities must be a key goal.

In a Canadian report, *From Restless Communities to Resilient Places*, the vision of development in Vancouver is held out as a model. 'Some mixes of housing are so successful that a visitor would be unable to tell the social housing from the market housing' (External Advisory Committee on Cities and Communities, 2006: 68). The report argues that the way land is developed should be part of well worked out strategies involving economic, environmental, social and cultural dimensions of sustainability – an interesting echo of the 'five pillars' of regeneration mentioned in Chapter 2. Community planning is vital, and yet proposed changes in our own planning regime do not seem to be encouraging this approach. One of the successes of the Wythenshawe work with Willow Park has been the ability of the trust to take a major, and in some cases a determinative, role in the whole future of the community. Where it has not had control – in the design of the new private sector development, for example – fences and walls have marked the continued existence of class and social divisions. There is a move in the Department of Communities and Local Government to delegate more power to local communities, with housing trusts playing a significant role. What is clear is that this must include private as well as social housing development and we must seek a hybrid or mixed-economy form of development.

In Milton Keynes, each new development has a 30% social housing element within it. It is impossible to distinguish between the two sorts of housing and means that there is a very real expectation that those in rented and owner-occupied housing will live side by side. Such a social mix is associated with the notion of 'hybridity' in works such as *The Mongrel City* (Sandercock, 2003), with its lack of pedigree and ethnic purity. Christopher Baker develops this model in *The Hybrid Church in the City* (2007). There is no reason why housing developments should not cater for an age-mix – such as supported housing for the young and the elderly. There should be housing for those with disabilities and mental illness. Building larger houses will prove attractive to many Asian communities, with the extended family providing an important part of their cultural tradition. Good community facilities in such developments become a necessity, whether it is religious space or meeting place. Aspirations would immediately be raised and poor educational opportunities would not be tolerated. Anti-social behaviour would become difficult as the middle classes show little signs of retreating into enclaves of fear despite the desire of the tabloids to label our communities as violent and lawless. Such communities should be given real power over their future and their residents' sense of well-being. These would be communities where black and white, young and old, the well-off and those struggling economically would be living side by side. Divisions of class would not be determined by where you live and what sort of house you lived in. Party political activity in such areas would have to be rethought, as old assumptions about political attitudes being determined by the area in which you live would be shattered.

We should be aiming for inclusive communities rather than the exclusive developments craved by the housing developers, who have so much influence with government. One of our greatest fears is that the massive housing development programme promised by the Government over the next twenty years will perpetuate these social and class divisions with the encouragement of the private sector. They will use the market to justify continuing to provide gated housing for the wealthy to protect them from the poor. This seems a total contradiction of the Christian vision of the Kingdom of God and a demonisation of those already excluded by the rich.

We are not only part of a nation divided by class and divisions imposed by housing availability. Each year the Institute of Fiscal Studies produces a survey of poverty and inequality in the UK. In the 2008 report they wrote:

> Breaking income down by region we find that median household
> income is highest in the South East, London and the East of England,

and lowest in the North East, West Midlands and Northern Ireland at about 91% of the UK median ... Income inequality has risen for a second successive year and is now equal to its highest-ever level ... Taking the period 1996–1997 to 2006–07 as a whole, incomes have grown fastest at the very top of the income distribution, as they did in the period of Conservative government that preceded it. Middle incomes have kept pace with incomes towards the top of the income distribution. However there is some evidence that incomes at the very top of the distribution have been 'racing away' from incomes further down the distribution. (Institute for Fiscal Studies, 2008: 1–2)

The Get Fair Campaign has drawn together a national coalition to end poverty in the UK. They remind us that 32% of children in the UK live in poverty; 17% of older people in the UK live below the poverty line; 43% of all UK adults are worried about their lack of money; and 30% of adults with a disability live in poverty. David Lammy MP, Minister for Skills, had been quietly lobbying for such a campaign for some time, as clearly his Christian socialism has been challenged by the failure of the Labour Government to make more of an impact on the divisions that exist in British society. He gave the Christian Socialist Movement Tawney lecture in 2007 and addressed the deep and widening divisions that scar our nation. He said:

> Just as Tawney himself did, we need to ask ourselves if we really treat every human life as if it has infinite importance. Can this be true in a society where the life chances of two children – born just one bed away from each other – can be so different? Not because of their talents, but because of their backgrounds? Or when life expectancy can differ so sharply not just from one country to another – or even one city to another – but from one part of one city to another? (Lammy, 2007: 5–6)

Attempts by local authorities to reduce these inequalities have at best been half-hearted. At least there is now no excuse for ignorance. The statistical material is available on almost every local authority and primary care trust website. The previous Labour administration in Sheffield made a bold attempt to move resources from the west side of the city to the east side where life expectancy was shorter by almost ten years. The political price for this is likely to be costly, however, as votes gained in the needier communities will be outweighed by those lost in the affluent areas, due to higher turnout in the latter in local elections. Sure enough, that Labour administration in Sheffield is no longer in power.

Divided by ... 'race'

In January 2008 the Bishop of Rochester, Michael Nazir-Ali, wrote an article for the *Daily Telegraph* that created an uproar. In it he attacked immigration of people of other faiths into the UK and the philosophy of 'multi-culturalism'.

> This required that people should be facilitated in living as separate communities, continuing to communicate in their own languages and having minimum need for building healthy relationships with the majority. Alongside these developments, there has been a worldwide resurgence of the ideology of Islamic extremism. One of the results of this has been to further alienate the young from the nation in which they were growing up and also to turn already separate communities into 'no-go' areas where adherence to this ideology has become a mark of acceptability. (Nazir-Ali, 2008)

It was difficult to find any justification for the Bishop's remarks. Multi-culturalism has been a model for community relations, but has been rightly subject to serious criticism and re-examination in recent times. Newly arrived communities have always sought the security of living near family members and friends, whether Jews, Poles, Irish, Caribbean, African, Chinese or from the Indian subcontinent. The availability of suitable housing, the welcome or lack of it of the host community and the proximity of familiar community facilities and social institutions are all going to influence patterns of immigration and settlement. The Bishop also seemed to forget the stories of the racism served up by the Church of England that greeted those Anglicans who arrived from the Caribbean seeking a welcome at churches in the 1950s and 1960s. Yasmin Alibhai-Brown, in a stinging rebuttal of the article in the *Independent*, quoted Professor Carl Peach of Oxford:

> Let us be clear, there is not a single ward in Britain in which the population is a hundred per cent ethnic ... there are several wards

where, if one aggregates all minority-ethnic populations they are the majority. However, 78 per cent of the minority-ethnic populations do not live in such wards. (Alibhai-Brown, 2008)

What is true is that immigrant communities are often found in the poorest parts of our cities, with low life expectancy, and encountering endemic racism. It is no coincidence that the British National Party's biggest successes have been in Barking, neighbouring on Newham and Waltham Forest, both boroughs with a high multi-ethnic presence. There can be little doubt that the rise in the BNP vote is a cry of frustration from the traditional white working-class supporters of Labour who have experienced deterioration in their economic and social well-being. Gordon Brown's cry of 'British jobs for British workers' acquired a sinister tone as recession began to bite.

Housing remains a major issue, with the right-to-buy policy removing almost 50% of council stock over the last 20 years. The Bishop of Barking noted at a meeting to discuss the election results that 'landlords shifting people around on short-term tenancies is a major problem'. 'This,' says Nick Lowles of *Searchlight*, 'alongside the borough having the lowest cost housing in London, has resulted in the greatest movement of people in the capital and made the job of rebuilding communities more difficult' (Lowles, 2008). The borough has the lowest average income in the capital. Adult basic skills are very low and levels of higher education qualifications the lowest in London. Barking and Dagenham is ranked fourth lowest nationally for adult literacy and second lowest for numeracy skills. It is also experiencing the fastest changing demographics in the country. In the 1991 census 96% of people described themselves as 'white'. This fell to 85% in 2001 and the Office for National Statistics estimated in 2003 that the white population was 76.3%. It is believed that the figure has now fallen below 70%.

Into this context there would reasonably be some expectation of substantial government help and intervention. Barking's contribution to the Thames Gateway development will not touch the lives of discontented Barking residents whose reliance on stable employment for the Ford's Dagenham works has been steadily eroded. Instead government schools investment was removed from the borough for their refusal to accept the academies programme. A few miles away, in North Newham, £billions are being invested in sporting facilities but little of the Olympic bonanza is likely to touch the lives of disaffected young people in Barking. Inequalities in the borough have risen and a growing discontent has both fed and been fed by the rise of the extreme Right.

The picture nationally mirrors Barking's story. Of the 25 wards that produced the best BNP votes in the last elections, almost all are among the 10% most deprived areas in the country. In places like Stoke-on-Trent and Barnsley the Labour vote has collapsed; in South Wales' Labour heartlands independents have swept to victory; and in Scottish constituencies the SNP have swept in although there is no apparent desire for Scottish independence. As Nick Lowles, in a very important article, puts it, the BNP is emerging 'as the voice of the forgotten working class':

> The BNP is tapping into political alienation and economic deprivation. It is providing a voice for those who increasingly feel ignored and cast aside by Labour. The BNP is articulating their concerns, grievances and even prejudices ... The clock is ticking and time is running out. The economic downturn, the credit crunch, the housing collapse and rising living costs are only going to increase insecurities over the next year or two. The political parties and in particular Labour, are letting down a large section of the British population. Without radical and immediate change, Britain could experience the political earthquake that is engulfing much of Europe. (Lowles, 2008)

In January 2009 Communities and Local Government produced a report from the National Community Forum on *Sources of resentment and perceptions of ethnic minorities among poor white people in England* (Garner, Cowles and Lung, 2009). Although based on a comparatively small sample, its conclusions confirm our own reflections:

> Two major if not particularly original conclusions ... are first, that community cohesion and integration are hampered most by poverty and related socio-economic issues; and second, local conditions are still very significant framing factors for any relationships between groups of people. (Garner, Cowles and Lung, 2009: 9)

The researchers also saw that people were happy to refer to themselves and their communities as 'working class', and the concerns they focused on are seen through a set of experiences that are clearly marked by class. 'Where immigration and integration are discussed in depth as problematic, there is a focus on real or perceived competition for resources; housing, benefits, jobs, territory and national culture' (Garner, Cowles and Lung, 2009: 41).

In fact, statistics clearly show that the Black and minority-ethnic communities in general are not flourishing at the expense of the white working class, and there is a call for better dissemination of information on resource allocation and migration. The report also calls for a proper debate and new understanding of what is meant by 'integration' in the 'community cohesion and integration' agenda, and the development of forms of local dialogues particularly around notions of 'political correctness'. Although mention is made of 'local groups' being involved in this process it is clear that local faith groups working together could play a significant and trusted role in enabling this sort of local dialogue. Removing the blinkers of policy-makers to the role of faith groups around community cohesion, and providing them with resources to engage in development, ought now to be on the agenda of central government.

Even Alan Billings' rather sceptical take on the capacity of faith groups 'to embrace pluralism not as a threat to God's plan for the world but an essential element in it' admits that they may have a role in advancing community cohesion (2009: 124). Whether it is community or associational churches, Billings believes that they may have a contribution to make to community cohesion. But it can be threatened in three ways:

> First when a community feels under threat and emphasizes religion as a marker for its identity; second when people of faith, who may feel insecure for other reasons, believe the position or the honour of their religion is threatened; and third, and most serious when believers persuade themselves that they have some form of divine mandate to forward their cause by any means, including violence. (Billings, 2009: 111)

With Billings we would want to argue for pluralism. As he says, 'pluralism protects from a stultifying uniformity'. But as we have seen throughout the book so far, there are a host of factors that contribute to the community that works, that makes for a good, safe, fulfilling place to live. As the NCF research pointed out, the economic and social divides that still bedevil many communities are a major factor in the way a pluralist society views its neighbours. 'Life is hard for me. Whom shall I blame for this?'

Divided by … a democratic deficit

This chapter began with stories from housing estates where the sharp inequalities that divide our nation are experienced most sharply. This has been aggravated by a growing fear of crime, of guns, knives and gangs. Anti-Social Behaviour Orders (ASBOs) have found their largest successes (or at least use) on Manchester's council estates. While life may certainly have improved for some local residents the process has done little to tackle the underlying problems that possess these estates. One experienced youth worker in Miles Platting in Manchester described the community as suffering from depression. Mums will deliver children to school in their nightclothes and pick them up in the afternoon still not dressed. At least gangs offer young people an opportunity for self-esteem and 'respect'. Drugs offer an escape from the cold.

What remains important is that the church is still there as a vital part of these communities, and maybe offering in some of them a beacon of hope. But it has to be more than a sticking-plaster presence, binding wounds and comforting the broken-hearted. It has to be transformative and visionary, offering a picture of the good city where all are valued unconditionally.

Can nothing be done? Polly Toynbee and David Walker have produced *Unjust Rewards* (2008). It is a savage analysis of the way in which government has allowed the rich to become richer, perhaps still subconsciously in the forlorn belief in the Thatcherite trickle-down model. Yet nobody believes that trickle-down works. The view that economic growth is dependent on the financial sector being untrammelled by regulation has to be re-examined in the light of recent recession and banking failure. Yet executive pay levels seem to be protected by the boards of both banks and companies. City lawyers defend salaries that are 100 times more than a teacher's. Toynbee and Walker tell the sorts of stories that are a commonplace to so many of the clergy working in our poorer estates. They point to the fatal effects of social exclusion and political apathy and issue an urgent call for change:

> Politicians must dare to say boo to the golden geese and regain their democratic authority. Within a generation or two a country could throw off dysfunctional inequality and enervating social discontent and become a fairer, less angry place.

Other countries have already been down this path. Most of the rest of Europe and especially the Nordic nations have been consistently more successful economically than the UK, yet have chosen to share the proceeds more fairly. Here, the case has been allowed to go by default. There really could be no poor children, none destined to fail from their first breath because of the family they were born into. (Toynbee and Walker, 2008: 228–9)

Yet when it comes to challenging the Government on these issues with the sort of prophetic ferocity that demands public attention there is still a strange reticence from the church's leadership. The Good Childhood Inquiry, set up by the Children's Society, has provided conclusive evidence in abundance of the failure of the UK towards its poorer children (Layard and Dunn, 2009). Government have certainly made some progress in efforts to eliminate child poverty. But fundamentally they have ignored the growing gap between the rich and poor. In fact they almost seem to glory in the 'wealth creators', as they have been described. These wealth creators have been exposed as leeches living off the credit-ridden body of the people of the UK. Poorer people have been encouraged to buy houses way beyond their means when the rented sector would have been much more appropriate, as is the case in the rest of Europe. Higher levels of debt have been encouraged so the banks could sustain their profit growth. Prophets such as Andreas Whittam-Smith (founding editor of the *Independent* and First Estates Commissioner) warned of disaster and were unheard even within the Church of England.

There is now an opportunity for real change. As Toynbee and Walker indicate the present recession may help serious soul-searching rather than further political posturing. It is time for the church to offer some real alternative vision about the sort of society we want for the twenty-first century. It is certainly a land where the people of South Oxhey and the Wye Estate do not experience a gap equivalent to the global North/South divide. It should be a land where young and old live life in all its fullness and rejoice in their neighbours.

We particularly want to suggest that the mark of an urban public theology should be to encourage the urban church to recognise the potential of its resources of 'faithful capital', the values and practices that enable it to live as an encouraging, inclusive and welcoming place. The church in South Oxhey is fundamentally hospitable, reflecting the ancient monastic tradition of sustenance, relief of poverty, and education. Yet the local church must model local ambition for a successful and integrated community. This has to mean that the local church has to rediscover ways of including those excluded by poverty, sickness, homelessness or illiteracy. The remarkable work done by many churches with the mentally ill is but one example of a trusted local organisation providing vital care and support for an often excluded group. St Luke's, Longsight, in Manchester, has a long and distinguished partnership with the local mental health trust, providing an 'open door' to many who would find it difficult to use more traditional day centres.

Lasting social cohesion is an often elusive ambition for government, an issue which we will discuss at length in our next chapter. But we suggest that the lack of a clear design of our urban space and a mixed housing economy has done much to damage community cohesion. The film *This is England* captures the bleakness of so many of our estates and the way in which stubborn social, economic, political and cultural marginalisation has contributed to the rise of the far Right. We welcome the massive investment in improving educational opportunities for those left behind in our educational system, but are only too aware of the ability of the middle classes to defend their territory against policies that might lead to more social integration. The greatest criticism of some parts of the church's contribution to education must be the exploitation by the professional middle classes of the 'church attendance rule' to gain entry to academically successful and often socially exclusive schools, thus contributing to a less balanced entry into neighbouring state secondary schools.

Finally, the 'democratic deficit', which we examine in Chapter 7, means that the pain of our divided cities is only a political issue when it impacts on those with greater wealth and influence. It is a sad reflection on the post-war era that major investment in our poorest communities has largely occurred after outbreaks of rioting and public disorder. There is a remarkable film produced by Oxfam, which interviews a group of well-off middle-class women in a Cheshire village, asking them whether they believe poverty still exists in Britain. The answer is a resounding 'no', yet every statistic shows that the gap between rich and poor has grown markedly in recent years, and, despite government policies, targets to eliminate child poverty are unlikely to be met. The 'democratic deficit', the political unimportance of the poorest in our divided cities because of their lack of participation has added to their social exclusion. Indeed it was a government minister, who is a practising Christian, who urged the churches to initiate a national 'Get Fair' campaign, replicating 'Make Poverty History', as the Government would welcome more political pressure about poverty at home. This was an area where *Faithful Cities* left no room for doubt. The elimination of poverty is a theological imperative, but political endeavour will only succeed where there is a coherent strategy to eliminate class divisions preserved by physically divided communities, disempowered and excluded groups and deep-seated despair.

5
From Babel to Pentecost

Introduction

The philosopher Aristotle is credited with the following saying: 'A city consists of differing kinds of humans; similar humans do not bring about a city' (*Politeia*). This chapter is about the cultural diversity of our urban communities, and how increasingly urban dwellers are inescapably touched by the phenomenon of globalisation. We ask whether diversity is to be feared or celebrated, and how the urban church should best respond in terms of facilitating faithful citizen-disciples, in embodying the divine values of hospitality and community, and in being a catalyst for mature, considered debate about the future of our multi-cultural cities in ways that promote the common good. These questions derive from the three practical tasks of Christian nurture, corporate identity and dialogue with the world; and we will consider in particular how a practical theology might be forged out of an engagement with two biblical narratives – the Tower of Babel (Genesis 11:1–11) and the day of Pentecost (Acts 2:1–36). These may provide some guidance for the urban church as it attempts to articulate a public theology and an ecclesiology of cultural diversity.

Recession and the crisis of multi-culturalism

In January 2009 the Bishop of Manchester invited the local authorities that make up the Diocese of Manchester to meet to discuss the likely impact of the recession on local communities and the contribution the Church of England might make to alleviate the worst of the pain. It was well attended with most of the authorities sending senior officers and in Manchester's

case the deputy leader as well. Each local authority presented their strategies for dealing with rising unemployment, rising debt and repossessions and homelessness. Some even presented their reports submitted to relevant council committees. But it was in the discussion that ensued that a common underlying and serious threat was introduced. 'Community cohesion' was at risk.

One of the characteristics of modern Britain is the 'blame culture'. When anything goes wrong from child abuse to road deaths, from MRSA in hospitals to a child drowning, somebody must be found 'responsible' and punished so 'that it may never happen to anyone else again'. Another victim has to be found to carry both society's corporate grief and guilt. As we discussed in Chapter 4, the fear that recession will provide a platform for those from the far Right to exploit the deep-seated and long-standing racism within British urban communities is real. The British National Party received 6.5% of the vote in the last local elections in the North West region – not far short of the 8% needed for the election of a Member of the European Parliament. The election of BNP councillors in white working-class and sometimes more socially affluent wards has often been based on slogans of 'they're taking our jobs' and 'they get priority on social housing', prejudices which have no basis in fact. Thus the collapse of the economy provides fertile ground for 'the blame game'. Bankers and financial institutions are too distant a target when unemployment strikes possibly up to 3 million, despite predictions that the financial services sector will be at the front of the jobcentre queue. There is little doubt, as ever, that it will be the poorest communities in the north of England that will suffer the most. In fact there is evidence that the manufacturing, building and service industries will be radically affected and the poorly paid will find the recession hardest to bear. The exposure of Asian workers being exploited with low wages and appalling working conditions not in the Far East but in Manchester reveals something of the underbelly of British employment practices.

At the Bishop of Manchester's meeting one statistic that stood out was the fact that in 2007 50.33% of the Muslim population in Greater Manchester were among the 10% most deprived; 71.68% were among the 20% most deprived; against 22.84% of the total population among the 10% and 36.8% among the 20%. The Muslim population is the most economically vulnerable and yet the fear is that they will carry 'blame' for 'taking our jobs'. Combined with rising Islamophobia built on the aftermath of

George Bush's 'war on terror' — although this is now being discredited in many quarters — this makes for a potentially incendiary mix for many of our local communities.

Cities have always been places of mobility and migration, and the physical and geographical movement of peoples brings new challenges of identity and belonging. Government's anxiety about 'social cohesion' needs further examination, however, since it reflects deeper values about what cohesive and harmonious cities might look like and how that might be achieved. But fundamentally, contemporary cities are crucibles of globalisation with the convergence of cultures and communities never before required to live in such close proximity. It would be surprising if this did not present challenges to our concepts of governance, identity and common purpose:

> Large cities in the highly developed world are the places where globalization processes assume concrete, localized forms. These local-ized forms are, in good part, what globalization is about. We can then think of cities also as one key place where the contradictions of the internationalization of capital either come to rest or conflict. If we consider, further, that large cities also concentrate a growing share of disadvantaged populations ... then we can see that cities have become a strategic terrain for a whole series of conflicts and contradictions. (Sassen, 2006: 198)

In other words, global cities are the crucibles of social change, manifested particularly in the pressures of migration and concentrations of divergent populations in one place, and yet often least capable of responding to such change due to their already overstretched and scarce resources.

The irresistible force and the immovable object

There's a saying that in polite society one should not mix religion and politics. At the beginning of the twenty-first century in the West, this is still the orthodoxy in terms of our understanding of the relationship between public life and religious faith; between secular reason and theological profession. Since the European religious wars of the sixteenth and seven-teenth centuries, and the emergence of the Western Enlightenment in Europe and North America, the consensus has been that the two should be kept separate. This has been enshrined in 'liberal' political philosophy, which has argued for a neutral public arena from which religion is prohibited, on the grounds that any profession of faith is essentially an encroachment on another person's freedom. From that point of view, it was argued, religion should be kept out of public life: the privileged position of Established Churches is an anachronism, there is no such thing as 'public theology' and religion is the enemy of social cohesion.

The classic perspective on this is often associated with the political philosopher John Rawls (1921–2002). Rawls' classic answer is that the public polity must be founded on a set of values and principles that reasonable citizens of a civil society could willingly and openly endorse as legitimate for the public forum on matters of constitutional essentials and basic justice. In public political debates, appealing to this common set of values and principles represents a co-operation on the basis of common reason and thus gives rise to civic friendship and mutual respect. Even if political or policy debate concerns matters of ethical and moral signifi-cance – such as abortion, stem-cell research, euthanasia, civil partnerships, even going to war – no publicly stated political discourse should rest on principles that are only accessible to a partial section of the community. Therefore, religious discourses and activities in a pluralistic society should be kept within the confines of the religious sphere. They should be found only in places that are properly theirs, such as in a church, temple, seminary or religious assembly. In other words, there is no justification whatsoever for beginning with one's own religious premises in a public forum. Public discourses in a pluralistic society should be grounded only on shared – that is, secular humanist – beliefs and norms.[5]

Former chairperson of the Humanist Society, journalist Polly Toynbee, is a vocal representative of a kind of 'new secularism' which attacks any religious intervention in public affairs and, by implication, denies any religious basis to multi-culturalism or national identity. In this extract, her response to the bomb attacks on Central London in July 2005, and to evidence that pointed to the radical Islamic influence on those who carried them out, is expressed as a call for the expulsion of all religion of any kind from public life:

> The death cult strikes again, unstoppable in its deranged religious mania ... This is not about poverty, deprivation or cultural dislocation of second-generation immigrants. There is plenty of that and it is passive. Iraq is the immediate trigger, but this is about religious

delusion. All religions are prone to it, given the right circumstances. How could those who preach the absolute truth of every word of a primitive book not be prone to insanity? (Toynbee, 2005)

Her view of religion reflects the Enlightenment thinking of figures such as Feuerbach, Marx and Freud, who dismissed religion as a collective and toxic delusion which would, fortunately, disappear as the world became more rational. The popularity of such views, also represented in the writing of Richard Dawkins, Christopher Hitchens and others, should be a salutary lesson for all representatives of organised religion, since it seems to resonate at some level with public sympathies. Yet Toynbee's view is crudely reductionist – religion alone must take the blame, no other socio-economic factor – and strangely *illiberal* in its assumption that all religion is, by its nature, extremist. Her description of religious texts as 'primitive' reveals her contempt for cultures other than her own. To counter the 'irresistible force' of religious extremism with an equally vituperative and intolerant 'immovable object' of secularism does nothing to advance greater understanding, either of the motives of those who fall under the influence of radical Islam, or of a way to build a more cohesive society.

Toynbee is not alone in her tendency to confuse the state of being 'religious' and being illiberal, as in the sense of failing to respect diversity or public debate. However, this may be to confuse the *origins* of certain kinds of strongly felt values with their *consequences*. Not only is it misguided to say that all religious doctrines are infallible, it is also arguable whether religious groups are any more passionate than secular groups in defending their beliefs. Can we actually sanitise our political and social institutions from the fact that human beings tend to be more passionate and even aggressive for what they care deeply about, whatever the foundations of such beliefs? On the contrary, Nicholas Wolterstorff warns that 'in our century, most have cared more deeply about various secular causes. It would be danger-ously myopic to focus one's attention on the danger that religion poses to the polity while ignoring the equal or greater danger posed by secular causes' (Wolterstorff, 1997: 112–13). In other words, why should some people be required to 'bracket out' their beliefs for the sake of a putative common good? In fact, it may be seen as a restriction of the freedom of some citizens to require them not to draw on their beliefs when it comes to contributing to political or moral debate.

Historically speaking, the incompatibility of religion and reason may not even be a particularly accurate representation of the emergence of Western modernity and resulting settlements over the separation of church and state. Stephen Toulmin argues that there never was such a polarisation between 'secular humanism' and 'Christian orthodoxy': many of the early modern scientists and political theorists were devout believers, and the introduction of principles of free speech and tolerance were never intended to exclude religious reasoning from public debate (Toulmin, 1990: 24–5). An Enlightenment critique of religious authoritarianism and the compulsory conjunction of church and state – and thus the enforcement of mandatory religious affiliation – should not be confused with the total redundancy of all religion. As José Casanova argues, 'secularisation' in that respect was about the 'emancipation' of the secular from the religious, but willed as much in the name of religious pluralism as the wish to see the end of all religion (Casanova, 1994). Casanova is critical of those versions of secularisation theory that conceive the process of secularisation as the inevitable and inexorable disappearance of religious beliefs and practices in the modern world or the ultimate triumph of scientific reason. He questions such versions of the secularisation thesis on both normative and empirical grounds, arguing that they simply perpetuate 'a myth that sees history as the progressive evolution of humanity from superstition to reason, from belief to unbelief, from religion to science' (Casanova, 2006: 17). This mythical account of secularisation, says Casanova, is itself in need of 'desacralisation'. Increasingly, therefore, notwithstanding the new secularists, the search is on for a way of relating religion and public life that reflects a world in which, despite the predictions of social theorists, religion has not disappeared, but has in fact experienced a startling new visibility throughout the world.

Writing for the Fabian Society, Sunder Katwala argues it is possible to defend principles of equality, fairness and freedom without necessarily arguing that any kind of religious reasoning or perspective is automatically a threat to that: 'It is now becoming increasingly clear that the more visible prominence of religion in … politics requires us to rethink and redraw the boundaries between religion, the state and public life' (Katwala, 2006: 246). We need to differentiate between two distinct principles of the liberal state: (1) the state should not privilege one form of religious expression over another; (2) religion should be kept entirely private. This is a fundamental confusion, argues Katwala, and leads to the assumption that 'religious citizens must abstract themselves from their deepest beliefs in accepting an iron distinction between private beliefs and public values' (2006: 248).

Katwala proposes two models of public debate: ideological secularism and pragmatic secularism (Katwala, 2006). The first seeks to maintain a hard-and-fast firewall between public and private, between reason and faith. The alternative, pragmatic secularism, would as a matter of principle value the rights of all citizens but refuses to discriminate on the grounds of religion, just as it seeks to respect diversity of gender, sexuality and ethnicity. This means it must respect the prerogative of religious participants to advance religious views in public.

In November 2006, Rowan Williams made a similar distinction between what he terms 'programmatic' and 'procedural' secularism. While programmatic secularism suspends any talk of value in a semblance of instrumental neutrality, procedural secularism engages with, but attempts to adjudicate between, competing convictions:

> It is the distinction between the empty public square of a merely instrumental liberalism, which allows maximal private licence, and a crowded and argumentative public square which acknowledges the authority of a legal mediator or broker whose job it is to balance and manage real difference. The empty public square of programmatic secularism implies in effect that the almost value-free atmosphere of public neutrality and the public invisibility of specific commitments is enough to provide sustainable moral energy for a properly self-critical society. But it is not at all self-evident that people can so readily detach their perspectives and policies in social or political discussion from fundamental convictions that are not allowed to be mentioned or manifested in public. (R. Williams, 2006b).

José Casanova himself has argued for the persistence of religiously motivated influences in the public sphere, and endorses the continuity of faith-based organizations' contribution to public life, so long as they are capable of acknowledging the pluralist nature of society. *If* religions react constructively to differentiation, *if* they do not work against the modern individual freedoms – Casanova argues – they can become legitimate public voices. However, it does still presuppose that society is made up entirely of those who desire social harmony, will listen to others, and will 'seek the common good'. It also implies that there is still some 'neutral' arbitrator or facilitator that can encourage religious groups to examine their own traditions and see how participation in such pluralist debates is thoroughly compatible with the teachings of their faith. So it seems that this IF is a BIG IF – does it still depend on religious world-views in some way being 'tamed' or moderated by Western Enlightenment standards of civility and pluralism? Who can adjudicate between the immovable object and the irresistible force?

So, on the one hand, there may be sources and resources that religion has to offer to a wider public debate, as a form of 'practical wisdom' that can enrich and nurture a healthy civil society. But, of course, this still flies in the face of a secularist insistence that religious people are incapable, as it were, of curbing their enthusiasm when it comes to reasonable debate. So it would seem that British society is stuck between a rock and a hard place: between the irresistible force of passionate religion and the immovable object of secular liberalism. Nevertheless, there may be a way through, not least by recovering voices of tolerance, respect and diversity from within the Christian tradition itself, and forging a praxis of citizen-discipleship that is nurtured by such a practical theology.

The Tower of Babel

The story of the Tower of Babel as related in Genesis 11:1–11 is a myth about the origins of cultural diversity, and in particular the multiplicity of human language. It tells of a mini Fall from the state of original uniformity, and at first glance the reader may ask why such human unity is not, seemingly, the desire of YHWH. The normative message is that a common language is wrong, and deserving of divine punishment, but further meanings need to be unpacked. The story tells of the settlement of a nomadic people, of migration into a single place and the grand design of a great metropolis. The building of the city is an expression of human ingenuity, serving as a testimony to the wonders of this civilisation (v. 5). Yet there is a danger that such achievements might threaten to usurp the authority of YHWH and tempt humanity to outstrip their finitude. So is this the action of a jealous God who will not countenance such insubordination – echoes, perhaps, of Genesis 2—3 where human curiosity and autonomy is also circumscribed?

Commentators debate as to whether YHWH's response to the building of the Tower is one of jealousy – to see off some potential rivals – or protectiveness – to save humanity from itself. Ellen van Wolde points out that the erection of a monumental tower that reaches to the heavens should not necessarily be read as humanity attempting to 'invade' into heaven and thereby dethrone the Almighty: 'it is not about the upward striving of human beings but about their horizontal striving: those people did not want to get to heaven or to God, but to remain on earth in one place' (van Wolde, 1996: 168). The ancients did not consider that God dwelt 'up there' in such a literal way. Rather, it is about the consequences of humanity's consolidation of its civilisation into one grand plan, symbolised by the dizzying audacity of a tall tower that seemingly defies gravity. For what people have lost is their rootedness and the contingency of feeling the specificity of that place: it is about an attempt to 'play God', not to defy divine edict so much as a denial of human creatureliness. The Tower offers the illusion of a view from nowhere, a universal, panoptic vantage-point that soars above the confusion of human difference. God's desire is for humanity to disperse and to inhabit the entire created world, to experience different habitats and environments, to relate in a dynamic and interactive fashion to the earth, rather than aim for a technologically driven 'transcendence' or be satisfied with the colonisation of one place alone.

Interestingly, YHWH's intervention, when it comes, occurs first in the form of seeing, moving and only then speaking (v. 5). YHWH enters the human space, but then, rather than destroying the edifice itself, simply 'scatters' the population. The divine will appears to be human diaspora and migration. The aspiration to human unity via one language is interrupted by a breaking of the unity of place.

However, is this a story that believes humanity is made not for diversity, but for separate development? Commentators insist that Genesis 11 is intended to reinforce chapter 10, in which human diversity is affirmed via the genealogy of nations. Rather than commending cultural separatism, the story is more interested in exposing the hubris of human attempts to embody the absolute. Culture is dynamic, just as humanity needs to remember its nomadic past even as it comes to settle and dwell; but equally, no human construction, no language, can tell the whole story. The view from nowhere, free of physical and spatial encumbrance, is an impossibility for humans – indeed, it is a form of blasphemy, since only God is One and free of such contingency.

A number of contemporary interpretations make a connection between the Tower of Babel and globalisation (Amos, 2004; Sacks, 2003). Jonathan

Sacks reflects on the challenges of multi-culturalism and the responsibilities of religion. In his own way, he is warning against the perils of the 'immovable objects' and 'irresistible forces' that set themselves up as the final answer, the universal truth that brooks no opposition, no dialogue. It is a warning against 'fundamentalism' of any kind! Speed of communication and the impersonality of modern life breeds lack of care or respect in engaging with difference: 'Gone are the days where people of different views were forced to share an arena and thus meet and reason with their opponents. Today, we can target those who agree with us and screen out the voices of dissent' (Sacks, 2003: 2).

Could we read Babel as an allegory of globalisation, or the supremacy of the market, or global brands, or even English as the predominant language of commerce and communications? A dominant culture such as that cannot easily tolerate rivals, or difference, and will resist threats to its hegemony. Mark Brett's 'post-colonial' reading sees Babel as an impertinent presumption of divine power, a quest for empire (Brett, 2000: 46). Clare Amos argues that Babel and its city is conceived out of a desire for security, and that this is what incites the construction of walls and defences. She recommends that we read Genesis 11 alongside Revelation 21:25, which speaks of a city without walls or barriers: 'The gates of the city shall never be shut by day, nor will be any night there.' Cities built out of fear, a desire for security, of the purity of the same, represent the imposition of monolithic rule. Sacks concurs: Babel is 'the first totalitarianism … It is the attempt to impose an artificial unity on divinely created diversity' (2003: 52).

Sacks repudiates the view that truth and certainty rest in unity and universality, a view he traces back to Plato's belief in the imperfection of the material, contingent world, although it is also reminiscent of Rawls' attempt to create a neutral, eirenic public sphere in which signs of difference are 'bracketed out' in order to achieve consensus. The logic of Sacks' argument may be that such consensus is sterile, even hubristic: 'What we cannot do is place ourselves outside the particularities of language to arrive at a truth, a way of understanding and responding to a world that applies to everyone at all times. That is not the essence of humanity but an attempt to escape from humanity' (Sacks, 2003: 54).

Ascending the Tower may appear to be a worthy exercise in rising above the argument in the interests of a more dispassionate perspective, but such a withdrawal is not a luxury available to us. The search for truth, and that of

God revealed in the process, remains at ground level. Translated into a dialogue between cultures and religions, Sacks is clear that diversity is not an impediment to, but the very territory in which, a recognition of our common humanity *takes place*:

> we need to search – each faith in its own way – for a way of living with, and acknowledging the integrity of, those who are not of our faith. Can we *make space for difference*? Can we hear the voice of God in a language, a sensibility, a culture not our own? Can we see the presence of God in the face of a stranger? (2003: 5; our emphasis)

While monotheism may appear to sanction absolute allegiance to an exclusive faith – 'I am a jealous God who will have no others before me' – Sacks argues that the covenant which is at the root of all Abrahamic traditions embodies respect for difference. It casts a sacred bond between humanity and the Holy One that endows human nature with an indissoluble dignity, even amidst difference. Evoking Martin Buber, Sacks asks: 'Can we find, in the human "thou", a fragment of the Divine "Thou"? Can we recognize God's image in one who is not in my image? There are times when God meets us in the face of a stranger' (2003: 17).

Implicitly, however, a form of exclusivism creeps into Sacks' analysis when he relates that, after Babel, the covenant continues, but is located in a special relationship with one nation, one culture in particular: 'God's covenant with humanity has not ceased. But from here on he [sic] will focus on one family, and eventually one people, to be his witnesses and bearers of his covenant … Theirs will be a singular and exemplary fate. They will be a people who are different' (2003: 52).

Such exclusivity is, however, challenged by a Jewish sect that emerged in the first century CE, initially in Jerusalem and then throughout the world, which believed that the covenant did not rest on one people alone. Hence Christians' tendency to see the story of the day of Pentecost (Acts 2:1–36) as a reversal of Babel. The covenant is renewed and proclaimed in the form of the Good News of Jesus Christ as the expression of God's reconciliation with the whole of creation; but what triumphs is not the restoration of a single *lingua franca* or the obliteration of cultural pluralism but human communication, and the gifts of the Spirit – which forge a Body of Christ that, similarly, finds its identity in interdependence amidst diversity. As the Spirit animates the disciples, they find themselves speaking in the tongues of all known nations and moving out into the public square to address the gathered citizens and visitors: an affirmation of the heterogeneous, enculturated and public nature of the Gospel.

Religious diversity in Aotearoa New Zealand

On a recent visit to Aotearoa New Zealand, Elaine was struck by attempts at the very uppermost levels of government to incorporate questions of faith into public life, and to acknowledge the significance of religious conviction and affiliation for many members of the community. Yet this was a long way from being the work of religious pressure groups or special pleading. Despite being a professed agnostic, the Prime Minister of the time, Helen Clark, gave personal endorsement and thus vital credibility to the Statement that was drafted by the Aotearoa New Zealand Human Rights Commission. It seems to have originated in a political debate that concluded that a healthy civil society that prided itself on its *cultural* diversity could not 'bracket out' the question of its members' *religious* diversity: 'Increasing religious diversity is a significant feature of public life … It is in this context that we recognise the right to religion and the responsibilities of religious communities … The right to religion entails affording this right to others and not infringing their human rights' (NZDAP, 2007: 3).

The Statement incorporates clauses on freedom of religion and belief, and guarantees the right to freedom from discrimination on the grounds of religious or other belief. It recognises that faith communities and their members have a right to safety and security, and employers and public services should take 'reasonable steps' to accommodate diverse religious beliefs and practices. Schools should teach an understanding of different religious and spiritual traditions in a manner that reflects the diversity of their national and local community.

If realised effectively in workable public policy, the Statement has the potential to depart significantly from the model of religion and the state contained within the classic liberal Western Enlightenment model. It does not envisage the neutral, secular state which suspends all references to religious affiliation in matters to do with citizenship, national identity and multi-culturalism; instead it understands that government has a positive responsibility to build and maintain positive relationships and to promote mutual respect and understanding. Yet as one commentator, Joris de Bres, remarks, such a statement does not contradict the non-partisan brief of the Aotearoa New Zealand Human Rights Commission, since 'the State has as much of a responsibility to engage with citizens who share a community of belief as they do with those who share a community of culture, ethnicity or geography' (de Bres, 2007: 9).

Supporters of such an initiative may argue, therefore, that by enshrining religious identity and affiliation in public policy, the government is taking a significant step to guarantee the parameters of social cohesion against the manifestations of religious resurgence globally. In the classic liberal segregation of religion and politics, as an ideal form of 'strong' secularism, all partisan values and principles, especially theologically derived ones, are to be insulated from the public domain. In a 'post-secular' world, however, such a distinction could actually militate against any kind of public transparency or accountability on the part of minority religious groups, by disallowing any common space in which religiously motivated policies could be debated. Neither secular states nor secularist public rhetoric are necessarily a protection against religiously motivated politics. Quite the opposite, in fact, if a residue or minority of religious parties takes on the mission of actively shaping the political or civic agenda. Without a statement on religious diversity that is both theological *and* political, New Zealand might find itself vulnerable to such a process. It is also an interesting echo of Sunder Katwala's position that the segregation of faith and politics may constitute a form of discrimination against those whose cultural backgrounds do not recognise such a distinction (Katwala, 2006).

In November 2008, Clark's Labour Government was removed from office in the general election and at the time of writing the future of the Statement hangs in the balance. Indeed, there are potential loopholes. There is little indication of how it might translate into firm public policy beyond broad statements about difference and respect. In fact, the initiative may be driven as much by the agenda of national security as by the broad principles of human rights. Whereas the authors of the report stress the value of interfaith relations and a statement such as this is a step towards 'learning the art of dialogue' between faith communities and wider society, Helen Clark's comments in her Preface betray a second concern. 'It is my hope', she stated, 'that the Statement will help all New Zealanders, of whatever faith or ethical belief, to feel free to practice their beliefs in peace and within the law' (NZDAP, 2007: 2). The Statement does contain some comment on people's right to practise religion free from harassment, and the need to address disputes between faiths, which might be sanctioned by legislation, but Clark's emphasis also reflects a tension between aspirations towards interfaith understanding and government anxiety about national security, social cohesion and religious extremism.[6] Nevertheless, it recognises that religion cannot be separated from all the other factors shaping civic and national identity:

> By now we should know that sustaining solidarity in a culturally and religiously diverse population is one of the foremost challenges facing nation-states today. As inward migration increases, many countries grapple with increasing discrimination, ethnic tensions, racism and violence, while simultaneously struggling to improve health, education, employment and immigration policies that stimulate social cohesion. A robust, culturally diverse population and the freedom of belief can therefore be strong indicators of a nation's internal security. Fostering public policies in support of these initiatives is therefore of utmost importance. Moving beyond mere tolerance of difference and into a sphere of active engagement is not only urgent, but also increasingly vital in today's global social climate as New Zealand manages the myriad issues arising from recent immigration and the continued growth of its cultural and religious diversity. Let's hope that we are up to the challenge. (Nachowitz, 2007)

It is worth continuing to follow the debate as it unfolds to see whether it represents a model for resolving the troubled relationships between the state, public reason and religious diversity. Such an initiative may be more achievable in a country the size of Aotearoa New Zealand (4 million), but it does represent a mature attempt to confront difficult questions about national identity, the role of history and the nature of citizenship in a post-secular context. The question is, would a government of whatever political complexion have the courage to open up such issues in the UK?

Renewing the vision

This is precisely what the Archbishop of York, John Sentamu, proposed when he spoke to the prestigious Smith Institute in January 2009. Recalling the contribution of William Temple to the Beveridge Report of 1942, Sentamu argued that the vigour and idealism of the proposals that went on to shape the post-1945 Labour welfare reforms puts the timidity and blandness of contemporary political debate to shame. The 'big vision' of justice, opportunity and social solidarity has, tragically, slipped our memories and has left us morally, as well as financially, bankrupt: 'Memory loss has made Britain sleep-walk on streets supposedly paved with gold, but sadly littered with promissory notes whose cash value is the credit crunch and the economic downturn as well as becoming a country that is not at ease with itself' (Sentamu, 2009: 3).

Government centralism and top-down initiatives have exhausted the capacity of communities to think and work inventively according to local needs and capabilities. A sense of shared national identity has been eroded and leaves us divided and demoralised. Despite government anxiety about 'social cohesion' – five major reports since 2001 – no real initiatives have been allowed to flourish, mainly because local communities have been starved of the power or resources to develop them.

Once more, therefore, Sentamu articulates the theme of a need to value localism and to trust grass-roots initiatives and communities. He also argues for a recovery of nerve on the part of faith communities to contribute actively to the debate about national identity. In proposing a threefold pattern for the churches' contribution to public life, Sentamu echoes Graham, Walton and Ward's stress on practices of discipleship that engender theological wisdom: promoting service as a core Christian ethic (nurture); living out Christian ideals in practice (corporate identity); and building up faithful capital for the sake of local communities and speaking out for the oppressed (public outreach). These are not done in ways that contravene the religious freedom of others, but rather in ways that seek to act out a public theology that 'practises what it preaches' and regards its vision of God as inseparable from its life in the world. Once more, this reinforces the spirit of *Faithful Cities* and endorses the thesis of *Moral But No Compass* by arguing that the essence of the church's contribution to public life is in the way it seeks to embody and live out its theology: it cares because it believes, and because *of what* it believes.

Conclusion

We have been stressing throughout this book the significance of space and place, both as a way of understanding the contemporary dynamics of urban life but also as a vital way of locating the vital witness of the urban church. Yet, paradoxically, one of the most marked features of globalisation is the gradual dissolution of the local as a discrete, unadulterated space. Increasingly, the local merges with the global: at the level of population migration, in terms of the 'flows' of capital, labour and commodities, in the weakening of the capabilities of the nation-state and in the 'hybridisation' of cultural identities. It is tempting for religious people to withdraw from these currents of history in the name of defending a faith that upholds purity and exclusive truth. Yet we have been arguing that a faith that allows itself to be shaped by biblical narratives will be called to proclaim a different sensibility. As Eduardo Mendieta argues, the greatest moral codes of human civilisation emerged out of such contexts of pluralism:

> Such codes arose precisely because individuals were thrown into the proximity of each other, and were thus confronted with each other's vulnerability and injurability. The injunction to take care of the poor, the indigent, the orphan, the widow, the invalid, could only arise out of the urban experience of the contiguity with the injurable flesh of the stranger. (Mendieta, 2001: 17)

Arguably, the continuation of such an ethic of hospitality and recognition of the other is all the more necessary if the protests of the new secularists against the incompatibility of faith and reason are not to become self-fulfilling prophecies. The globalised, multi-cultural cities are crucibles of new civilisations in the making, and the privilege of urban living is that it enables us to respond to the call of moral responsibility to our neighbour, to glimpse the face of Christ in that of the 'other' and to participate in the building of the new Jerusalem.

6
Cities of Culture

Introduction

The year 2008 was a good one for the city of Liverpool. An estimated 3.5 million visitors, generating around £176 million, were attracted to the city to mark its status as the European Capital of Culture. World-famous artists such as Paul McCartney, Ringo Starr, Simon Rattle, Terence Davies and Phil Redmond returned to the city of their birth to participate in high-profile events; but other attractions, such as a giant mechanical spider, 'Superlambanana' statues, a Tall Ships race and many exhibitions and community activities, also contributed to the cultural buzz. Yet 2008 reignited debate about the role of the arts in promoting urban regeneration after generations of economic decline. It was clearly a success, but since the designation of Glasgow in 1990 as the first British city of culture, the role of cultural industries in economic renewal has been a contentious one (Schopen, 2009). In this chapter, we will consider how debates about the role of 'culture' in urban regeneration relate to the analysis we have advanced about the state of our towns and cities. Can cultural regeneration deliver sustainable economic growth, and who benefits from such a process? What kind of regeneration strategies are implied by the Cities of Culture initiatives – what vision of 'the good city' do such programmes represent? And what is the role of the urban church in such revitalised 'cities of culture'?

As we discussed in Chapter 2, one of the main preoccupations of *Faithful Cities* was the question of what values, and whose interests, informed urban regeneration. Much of the criticism it advanced of government-driven urban regeneration projects focused on the way they often appear to be series of top-down 'initiatives' imposed on local people and neighbourhoods, which emphasise high-profile and prestigious developments at the expense of long-term sustainability or provision for the many. Similarly, criticisms of strategies to use the performing arts and other cultural activities to revive declining local urban economies express ambivalence towards its long-term effects, arguing that it represents a commodified and instrumentalised vision of culture at the expense of more inclusive, 'bottom-up' models of wealth creation and neighbourhood renewal.

We will explore how one key idea in *Faithful Cities* – that of 'faithful capital' – might foster a positive and proactive role for the urban church in this respect. While the church should be wary of the commodification of culture, it should not shy away from celebrating the many benefits that accrue from opportunities to foster human creativity, artistic endeavour and play as a God-given activity.

Regeneration and Cities of Culture

The debate about the relationship between culture and urban regeneration is not new. It all started in the 1980s, when politicians within the European Union decided that the so-called 'cultural industries' might be brought to bear in economic regeneration. The first British city to win the award was Glasgow, which was designated European City of Culture in 1990 (Mooney, 2004). Elaine remembers visiting an exhibition entitled 'Glasgow's Glasgow' which traced the city's history from the Industrial Revolution and the building of the shipyards, to industrial decline and revival. Her earliest years were spent in the 1960s near to an overspill town in Lanarkshire, which housed people from Glasgow, and she remembers being taken on the last tram by her parents in about 1962. In 1990, those very same trams were 'museum pieces': an example of how lived experience is transformed into heritage, even within a generation. In 1990, however, there was great controversy over whose version of the city's history was being related: critics argued that the occasion was more about encouraging corporate inward investment than celebrating Glasgow's working-class history, and especially that of popular culture and progressive politics (Mooney, 2004). As we shall see, this is a debate that continues to this day.

The year of 1990 was regarded as a success for Glasgow, however, and culture-led regeneration became enshrined in national and local government policy towards the UK's major post-industrial cities. Competition for the 2008 nomination was fiercely contested between Liverpool, Birmingham, Bristol, Cardiff, Newcastle-Gateshead and Oxford.

Meanwhile, following a paper by the Culture Secretary at the time, Tessa Jowell, on *Government and the Value of Culture*, in May 2004 the debate reopened on the role of the arts in society and, in particular, its potential for stimulating economic growth. It is interesting to note that Jowell's paper argues strongly for quite an intrinsic understanding of culture in society:

> Complex cultural activity is not just a pleasurable hinterland for the public, a fall back after the important things – work and paying tax – are done. It is at the heart of what it means to be a fully developed human being. Government should be concerned that so few aspire to it, and has a responsibility to do what it reasonably can to raise the quantity and quality of that aspiration. (Department of Media, Culture and Sport, 2004: 7)

Notwithstanding these comments, Jowell's paper has given rise to a view of the arts and culture in largely instrumental terms, related to their effectiveness in generating urban renewal and community development. The mainstream view is that the arts (as widely conceived) are, or should be, an integral part of the urban regeneration process and can also be an important element in promoting community development. These views are strongly evident in the debate about Liverpool becoming European Capital of Culture in 2008. Liverpool City Council hoped that the status of European Capital of Culture in 2008 would encourage a similar 'make-over' of public image as occurred when Glasgow won in 1990 (Centre for Cultural Policy Research, 2003). It is that all-important public image that is seen as central to enhancing a city's profile, and therefore its attractiveness to new business, new residents, tourists and a city's own population. Now, the Government has announced that it will launch a domestic equivalent of the European competition, so that a 'British Capital of Culture' will be awarded every four years. Andy Burnham, then Culture Secretary, commented: 'By receiving national recognition as a city of culture, any city of the UK could be given an opportunity to bring out the creative skills, talent and enthusiasm of its people – and showcase it on a national stage – and change perceptions of it' (Wintour, 2009).

Broadly, therefore, local and regional regeneration strategies have come increasingly to rely on cultural and creative industries as key drivers of economic revival and growth. In the context of the long-term collapse of manufacturing industry, culture becomes an important alternative source of 'urban entrepreneurialism' (Wilks-Heeg and North, 2004: 306). Landmark architectural developments, such as Liverpool ONE, Tate Modern in London, the Baltic in Gateshead and the Lowry in Salford, give a significant focus, as do sporting events: the 2002 Commonwealth Games for Manchester and the 2012 London Olympics. The potential of cultural events to attract tourists and raise the public profile of a place – even to redress stereotypes of dreary northern cities – is a clear benefit. It also brings with it new investment in transport infrastructure. So the growth of the cultural sector is also seen as part of a longer-term regeneration, in which the cultural industries themselves continue to buoy up the local economy; but it is the success of 'culture' to attract a particular kind of long-term resident that has proved the most compelling reason. For it is influentially argued that a strong cultural economy is crucial for creating the kind of dynamic, multi-cultural and competitive city that will flourish in the new global context.

Much of this is associated with the work of economist Richard Florida, Professor of Public Policy at George Mason University, Washington DC, who regards the growth of a 'creative class' as at the root of economically successful cities (Florida, 2002). Florida has argued that successful urban regeneration depends on a critical mass of 'creative' professionals in areas such as the arts, IT and education. Investment in attracting such 'creatives' pays more dividends than other strategies such as transport infrastructure, and cities should attend to attracting and retaining such high-octane talent if they are to succeed economically. If a city is vibrant culturally, then this will serve as a magnet to business and industry, resulting in an upturn in economic fortunes. It amounts to a conscious creation of a 'bohemian' subculture, which tolerates difference, alternative lifestyles and cultural innovation. This has been enthusiastically adopted by the British regeneration sector: in May 2003, Demos and the British Urban Regeneration Association (BURA) organised a conference entitled 'Boho Britain', and invited Florida as a keynote speaker (Demos, 2003; Carter, 2003).

Incidentally, Manchester topped the league of 'boho' cities in the UK, and perhaps epitomises the ambition of cities of culture with its attempts to deploy its undoubted cultural assets in industrial heritage, sporting achievement and artistic excellence to spearhead an extended period of post-industrial economic and social recovery that is now well into its second decade. It was also the logic that helped to spur the merger of the Victoria University of Manchester and UMIST in 2004 as part of a conscious effort to consolidate the 'knowledge capital' that a city such as Manchester is reputed to possess by virtue of its history of innovation in science, technology, medicine and the arts. So 'culture' has a wider meaning than simply the creative and performing arts, to embrace cities' heritages of built environment, sport and tourism as well as education, research and development, not to mention the ancillary industries to service the tourists, students and new workers that also contribute to a city's economic viability. As the short-listed cities competed for the award of the 2008 Capital of Culture, estimates of job creation ranked highly among their criteria. Bidding for Newcastle-Gateshead, the Regional Executive Director of Northern Arts commented, 'Capital of Culture status would enable the North East to deliver a cultural equivalent of the industrial revolution' (quoted in Wilks-Heeg and North, 2004: 306).

Manchester's cultural strategy

Exploiting the boho culture and its reputation for 'creativity' has indeed been an integral part of Manchester's regeneration strategy, as an arm of economic growth but also as a way of benefiting the local population:

> Manchester's Cultural Strategy ... places culture at the heart of the city's Community Strategy and Strategy for Neighbourhood Renewal. It is a vision led by the Council and offers a framework through which public, private and voluntary sector partners can work together towards common objectives. It covers a wide range of activities including arts, sports, tourism, heritage and media. (Manchester City Council, 2006)

It seems to us, however, that this also signals a new era in the scope and objectives of local governance. The days are gone when the provision of social services, housing, education, transport, environmental health and civic amenities such as libraries and swimming pools were considered to be the limit of city councils' intervention in the lives of their citizens, and that raising revenue was purely to fund such services. Today, councils are at the forefront of efforts to regenerate their local economies, brokering partnerships between the business, public and voluntary and community sectors. And economic regeneration is more than simply getting manufacturing industry, or even light industry such as retailing, to relocate to your city: now, city authorities wax lyrical about the 'new knowledge economy', the importance of 'quality of life', and the capacity-building potential of creative and cultural industries.

Similarly, as *Faithful Cities* noted, the growth of a regeneration 'industry' involves the blurring of public and private. City councils are engaged in the marketing of cities to win the contests for public (or EU money) such as City of Culture competitions, while private management companies are contracted to consult with local communities on schemes of local redevelopment, or of the use of parts of the community and voluntary sector to deliver public-sector services. That gives rise to issues of accountability, which we explore later.

But the attempt to use 'culture' as a tool for economic growth is open to criticism on a number of fronts. The main question is whether the arts, and culture more generally, can make a sufficiently lasting impact on local economies ravaged by urban decay, de-industrialisation, poverty and crime; a process of decline that may have been taking place over half a century or more. Certainly the public image of a city can be changed for the better, with places such as Glasgow, Manchester and Liverpool as good examples. But to what extent is that success a marketing tool, all the better to promote the city as a likely option for further inward investment, rather than any intrinsic strategy about culture as a generator of substantial new economic activity in its own right? And are the fruits of any resulting wealth creation equitably distributed? Do local communities living in the reinvented city benefit from living and working in a Capital of Culture?

Quantitative socio-economic statistics do not paint a particularly encouraging picture of such organic or integrated social regeneration. On the one hand, in Manchester, there have been thousands of jobs generated in the culture sector, and there is the undoubted proliferation of cultural choices for the consumer, plus the undoubted buoyancy of the city following the Commonwealth Games in 2002, both in public perception among its residents as well as further afield. Yet these have to be placed alongside the fact that Manchester still has very high morbidity and mortality rates, with one of the youngest average male mortality rates in England.[7] It is ranked as the least equal city in England (Centre for Cities, 2009). As the British economy entered recession in 2009, *Cities Outlook*

2009 (Local Government Association, 2009: 11) commented, 'Regeneration areas, which have offered high returns to investors in recent years, significantly underperformed the market as a whole during 2007.' Overall, *Cities Outlook* is pessimistic about the ability of large-scale regeneration programmes to generate corresponding reductions in inequality or deprivation. Similarly, in terms of widening participation and greater access to cultural industries, the jury is still out, with many still talking about the 'elitism' of cultural events. The evidence is indeed ambivalent, with costs and benefits equally balanced.

The strategy of municipal authorities promoting cultural regeneration by forging partnerships with corporate business, of deliberately pursuing a cultural 'make-over' of a formerly depressed city in order to attract inward investment, has prompted urban geographer David Harvey to reflect on the blurring of the boundaries between the market, the state and civil society we alluded to earlier (Harvey, 2008). He notes, first, the commodification of the city, as brand or marketing icon, but is concerned that this agenda results in attenuated and disengaged practices of citizenship:

> Quality of urban life has become a commodity, as has the city itself, in a world where consumerism, tourism, cultural and knowledge-based industries have become major aspects of the urban political economy. The postmodernist penchant for encouraging the formation of market niches – in both consumer habits and cultural forms – surrounds the contemporary urban experience with an aura of freedom of choice, provided you have the money ... This is a world in which the neoliberal ethic of intense possessive individualism, and its cognate of political withdrawal from collective forms of action, becomes the template for human socialization. (Harvey, 2008: 31–2)

Harvey is asking, essentially, what vision of the city is contained within the elevation of property values, boutique lifestyles and cultural assets, and whether it overwrites other dimensions of urban life, such as collective action, political participation and pursuit of social justice. As critics of Glasgow and Liverpool's cultural experiments also argued, the pressures of conforming to market-driven success marginalises alternative narratives or paths of engagement with public life, especially if public space is organised around the needs of the market and not insurgent culture. 'Lifestyle' displaces other models of citizenship. Harvey also describes how slum-

dwellers are removed from land to make way for lucrative property developments in the Two-Thirds World; elsewhere, 'undesirables' such as homeless persons or street hawkers can be moved off the streets during significant sporting events or cultural festivals. Such reminders of the underside of economic development disrupt the seamless narratives of 'salvation by shopping'; but is there a danger that the civic and democratic responsibilities of local government are subsumed under the interests of property developers and corporate finance?

The success of 'boho cities' depends on careful image-management, 'a massive rebranding exercise ... that revolves around cultural and architectural plans designed to send out a message that the city in question is a tolerant, convenient, but also exciting and pleasantly countercultural environment in which to live, work and play' (Baker, 2007: 35). This is 'City Lite', reminiscent of the 'heritage' city which has been air-brushed in the interests of presenting an uncomplicated version of the past, 'something that approximates to an original product ... but with the unhealthy bits taken out' (Baker, 2007: 35). Yet not only are the undesirable parts of a city's story edited out, but significant sections of a population may find themselves excluded, if their skills or self-presentation are deemed unsuitable (Mellor, 2002).

Clearly, therefore, cultural regeneration strategies have not been without their critics. There is concern that prestigious landmark projects, while attracting the lion's share of resources, are often merely pieces of 'window-dressing' that do little to transform the everyday lives of local residents. There is scepticism that landmark buildings and creative activity necessarily delivers a more successful or sustainable local economy. When it comes to high-profile 'signature' building developments, some cultural commentators have added to the controversy by attacking the quality of the developments on offer, arguing that the buildings are more valued for their appearance than their substance. The prime example here is the Millennium Dome, which was attacked for its overblown ambitions for the regeneration of Docklands.

Similarly, much of the regeneration money in Liverpool and Newcastle came from external sources, such as the European Union's (EU) regeneration fund, and had little to do with new businesses or artists actually generating new wealth organically as a result of new economic activity, in the shape of increased investment or consumer expenditure. Although Glasgow is regarded by many as the exemplar of creative and sustainable urban renaissance, following its year in the City of Culture spotlight in 1990, much of the funding that revitalised the area arrived long before the city even decided to make a bid for the title; and there is evidence that many of the projects, far from having a long-term economic impact on residents' lives, actually left the city council with substantial debts (Bianchini and Parkinson, 1993; Lally, 1991; Mooney, 2004).

Regeneration schemes have also proved divisive within local neighbourhoods, with negative effects on social cohesion, since the processes of 'gentrification' they trigger often price long-standing residents out of the area. This is something we analysed in *Faithful Cities*, particularly in the disruption that can be caused by the creation of so-called 'gated' communities out of former public-sector housing (CULF, 2006: 19, 3.16).

From this perspective, therefore, judging the value of culture according to economic and political criteria does little to aid the development of a genuinely high quality cultural life. And when it comes to boosting growth, can a few new art galleries or nightclubs match serious economic reform and investment as a driver for growth? Is it the case that 'culture' has been used as a pawn in a wider political game, but has little value as a means of genuinely improving the quality of life for anyone but a small wealthy minority?

Comments about Liverpool's year of culture posted on the BBC website expressed a range of views from the sceptical to the euphoric, and while we make no claims for their representative nature, it is interesting to see how they span the breadth of opinions already surveyed:

> 'It was just another year for me. Town centre gota face lift which was longer overdue, but apart from that what did the wider community of liverpool get out of it? nothing for the kids or the poorer communities. But the face lift will hide all those poorer and run down area's.'

> 'You do not help deprived areas simply by throwing a wad of cash. It needs continuous investment and a committment [sic] to a vision of how the city should develop.'

> 'What's the point of spending all the money on culture when it could have gone to deprived areas. Liverpool certainly has a North South divide, it's a shame!!! What a waste!'

> 'The superlambananas and the spider were great family entertainment. All capital of culture activities seemed so well planned and executed.

The organisers [sic] certainly made the most of the year, put Liverpool on the global map and gave us all something to be really proud of!' (BBC Liverpool, 2009)

So there is a tension at the heart of Britain's regeneration strategy. While everyone agrees that culture is a good thing intrinsically, there is scepticism that it has caused a significant upturn in economic growth, wealth redistribution or community renewal. Yet some would argue that if culture isn't delivering the anticipated urban renaissance, the problem lies with the kind of culture on offer.

Many commentators would argue that regeneration through cultural enterprises needs to come from the grass roots, rather than being centrally controlled by 'top-down' processes co-ordinated by quangos and other official bodies. Indeed, Sir Jeremy Isaacs, chairman of the expert panel who determined the winner of the City of Culture bid, has stated that one of the reasons Liverpool was named as the winner for 2008 was precisely because 'there was a greater sense there that the whole city is involved in the bid and behind the bid' (BBC *News*, 2003). Only if this is the case, runs the argument, will any particular initiatives translate into long-term, broad-based sustainable programmes of regeneration.

In the Executive Summary of its original bid, Liverpool boasted that its cultural map 'is grounded in the experiences of traditionally under-represented groups and individuals'.[8] So an interesting recognition here that, first, culture is a contested term, that it never comes from nowhere, and that, second, issues of participation and ownership are crucial matters to consider. The argument is that culture is not just about landmark buildings, but also about consultation and participation in order to connect with local people's aspirations. A community arts regeneration project 'from below', as it were, might have a very different complexion than the large flagship cultural enterprises that capture media attention.

Elaine is an avid supporter of the Victoria Baths renovation project in South Manchester, the Edwardian swimming pool and Turkish Baths that won the first BBC TV *Restoration* programme in 2003. It appears that it has been very successful in capturing public support because it has always been regarded as 'the people's palace', a place that people remember visiting, and so it continues to occupy a prime place in people's affections (P. Williams, 2004: Lock and Henner, 2006).[9] Eric Antones, head of Antwerp as City of Culture in 1993, has been reported as telling those responsible for Liverpool 2008 not to feel pressurised into pursuing an agenda of 'high culture' at the expense of fostering its local popular artistic heritage – such as the Beatles – in putting together its programme of artists and events (Teasdale, 2006: 4).

This probably only works if you have something as internationally lucrative and attractive – and so identifiable with the city – as the Beatles. But official promotion of small-scale, local culture doesn't necessarily deliver the goods of regeneration as local authorities and business interests would like. While the authorities are in a position to fulfil ambitious projects and create impressive landmark projects, centralised attempts to promote neighbourhood initiatives – be it oral history projects, photography exhibitions or poetry readings – could backfire and be seen as a cynical attempt to cash in on the remnants of a city's spontaneous cultural life. Neither will such a strategy necessarily attract vast numbers of outside visitors or encourage significant inward investment. Must we trade 'sustainability' for 'authenticity' therefore?

Cultural regeneration and the urban church

In terms of linking with the cultural agenda, faith-based organisations are often quite invisible when it comes to 'marketing' a city. Manchester's information on its cultural strategy speaks of diversity but there's little if anything about *faith* or *religion*. The only way in which the physical assets of faith-based organisations have been harnessed as a significant cultural asset is in the 'gentrification' of urban housing, although the vision of regeneration it presents may not be quite what most congregations have in mind.

For example, one regeneration strategy in parts of inner-city Manchester has been to buy up redundant church buildings to convert into state-of-the art 'executive apartments'. Theological language is deployed to create a sense of distinctiveness and desirability in the minds of prospective purchasers: religious heritage becomes a distinctive selling-point, creating an attractive ambience for the customer. For example, the estate agents Bridgfords have marketed the apartments created from the renovation of St Mary's Church, Hulme, as follows:

> A SENSE OF ENLIGHTENMENT – Moving away from today's 'usual' building conversions: residents of the church will be enveloped in the sense of history that emanates from every brick and beam ... The result is a living space that will touch your soul with its ambience, elegance and style.

> BE INSPIRED – The Church at St. Mary's has inspired those who
> have lovingly refurbished it ... Let it be your inspiration for life ...
> Find your Sanctuary in the City.[10]

So does faithful capital mean little more than 'sanctuary' for the stressed-
out middle classes? One of the risks for the urban church is that its potential
contribution to 'culture' becomes pigeon-holed into a particular form of
'heritage'. The so-called 'heritage industry' is perhaps another dimension
of culture as economic driver, since it represents a conscious marketing of
historic sites, buildings and other attractions – including religious sites – in
ways that make the teaching of history more accessible to tourists. The
heritage industry in this respect is more like geographical tourism, 'except
that in this case the travel is to past times. The past is a foreign country
where they do things differently, but we nevertheless holiday there,
returning to the safety of home when we choose to, and especially if the
situation becomes threatening' (Lewis, 2004: 31).

As Christopher Lewis warns, however, the intention may be to package
history in such a way as to render it palatable, with the result that it comes
to represent a particular, perhaps sanitised and selective, construction.
Hence the dilemmas facing cathedrals and other historic religious sites, but
perhaps by extension any local congregation seeking to participate in
cultural initiatives. What is expected of the urban church on the part of
those who sponsor and patronise such cultural events? It may be a desire for
nostalgia, or comfort, or profit, rather than an 'authentic' appreciation of
the role of an historic building, or even the faithful witness of a community, to the unfolding story of that place. Even worse, it may obscure the
fact that a building and congregation has a present and a future, as well as a
past.

So we come to the question of the connections between 'faithful capital'
and cultural agenda as part of urban regeneration. Many of the same issues
are there: of whose 'agenda' drives such programmes, and whether prestigious property-driven initiatives, however successful in boosting the local
economy, often prove less effective in delivering long-term material
improvement in the quality of life (however that is assessed) for its local
inhabitants. So clearly there is a danger that the resources and energy of
faith communities could often be 'co-opted' by the authorities, or the
capacities and skills of local people undervalued, in the process of regeneration.

This is consistent with *Faithful Cities'* contention that faith is often misunderstood by policy-makers and those steering regeneration projects. We have already made the case, however, for 'faithful capital' as finding expression in forms of critical partnership: not just acquiescing with the requirements of the regeneration industry, but retaining an autonomy and independence founded on the independent values of creation, human dignity and right relation. In that respect, to locate the urban churches and other faith-based organisations, sociologically speaking, as independent of both the (local) state and the market provides it with critical space in which both to forge partnerships and to cultivate independence, and to strive for a good compromise between honouring the demand for heritage, 'yet not to be swamped by it' (Lewis, 2004: 36).

Most local faith-based organisations would regard their 'faithful capital' as influencing their neighbourhoods in rather different ways. For example, *Faithful Cities* stresses that the strongly local nature of most faith-based organisations, which is often very longstanding, encourages a commitment to people and places that is tolerant of slow progress and assigns importance to building relationships and meeting the needs of specific people and groups. Another theme is to challenge very economically driven models of wealth creation, to ask questions about happiness and well-being: at what cost to our health, our environments, or our public life is the pursuit of economic growth or consumerism? Similarly, faithful capital draws on visions of an equitable society: to ask how government policies benefit the poor and marginalised; and to seek ways of empowering people (CULF, 2006: 30–44). This reinforces the case for a grass-roots approach to decision-making and community participation that values human flourishing and a rounded sense of what makes a good city, as well as models of wealth creation that pay attention to matters of equity and fair distribution. Culture is not something to be merely consumed; and it 'adds value' to our experiences of the city in ways that transcend the narrowly economic.

How might the urban church think theologically and act effectively in the light of this? *Faithful Cities* picks up on the idea of valuing the experiences and aspirations of ordinary people, recognising that often the agenda of urban regeneration is not driven with those interests at its heart. Yet it is not necessarily the task of Christian theology to oppose all attempts to boost a city's pride, let alone its economic well-being, through cultural renaissance. So there is some thinking to be done about 'culture' and its role in the building of the good city.

It is worth going back to the origins of the term itself. As Tim Gorringe reminds us, 'culture' is related etymologically to 'cultivation', in the sense of the application of labour to the natural environment to create fertile and productive land for pasture – agri-culture (Gorringe, 2004: 6). Just as humanity 'cultivates' the fields, so we also cultivate our minds. It is one of the processes that distinguishes humans from other animals, who may be capable of manipulating simple tools or building shelters, but who do not create sophisticated built environments with complex networks of trade, exchange and governance, as well as inhabit rich symbolic worlds of language, meaning and religion. As Gorringe says, therefore, culture is 'what we make of the world, materially, intellectually and spiritually' (2004: 12).

This is a lesson in learning to appreciate the significance of culture as one of the things that makes us human. In theological terms, it may be regarded as one of the signs of our image and likeness to God. It is important, therefore, that the common life of a city is enlivened as much by beauty as the creation of wealth. In Charles Dickens' novel *Hard Times* (1853), set in the northern industrial city of Coketown, he juxtaposes the rational, calculated, technical, managerial world of Josiah Bounderby and Thomas Gradgrind, the factory owners, and the more spontaneous, imaginative, colourful and joyous world of a circus, in which the sensibilities and values of childhood and play are well to the fore. Dickens may also have been suggesting, however, that Coketown is incapable of redemption: it is portrayed as a place of captivity, a contemporary Babylon, whereas the countryside around is one of innocence, like a Garden of Eden. Does this imply that the city cannot be a place of beauty, fulfilment and celebration? We should not pour scorn on the vision of the Cities of Culture movement to render urban spaces beautiful as well as functional. 'Culture' as an arm of regeneration must be a part of the good city, since it reminds us of humanity's spiritual aspirations and the role of culture in making meaning as well as wealth (Gorringe, 2004). This is about 'refreshing the soul' as much as rejuvenating the local economy (D. Ward, quoted in Miles and Paddison, 2005: 837) and perhaps of breaking down the barrier between work and industry as utilitarian and ugly, and leisure (the scarce commodity of the privileged few) as the superior path to well-being and fulfilment.

So the urban church, in its public theology of cultural regeneration, can afford to celebrate the best of culture as pointing towards human self-transcendence and to the divine origin of all beauty. Yet theological traditions of social justice and a preferential option for the poor, and a caution towards human perfectibility as attainable in this world, must give that endorsement a critical edge. This is where the worlds of 'Christ' and 'culture' have to be held in tension. This may entail monitoring the implicit values embedded in culture, and' choosing those of inclusion, agency and integrity 'as both working slogan and political ideal' (D. Harvey, 2008: 40). Does culture point towards a city of inclusivity and dignity; is it honest about sin and redemption, by refusing to 'edit out' the ambivalence of the human condition; is it realistic about the long-term sustainability of 'signature' events and developments?

Similarly, in its active promotion of cultural expression, the urban church as institution can do much to act as welcoming host. Its physical presence in every neighbourhood reminds society of the religious foundations of culture, not as a museum piece but as 'living stones' embedded still in space and place. It can foster culture as source of identity and pride, perhaps sponsoring projects – by young people or minority groups – under its own auspices that are not sufficiently attractive to corporate or municipal patronage. This is also linked to the question of harnessing and valuing the 'social capital' or 'faithful capital' of such communities, since cultural events would be highly effective means of capacity-building.

Yet a public facet of the urban church must also be its prerogative to challenge the vision contained within the grand programmes of civic renewal: on what is this house of culture standing – on sand, or solid rock? And since material culture, whether it be a landmark building or an arts festival, is always in some way a reflection of deeper spiritual values – what we value and what we worship – then the urban church can do well to return to that perennial question as a barometer of cultural industry's contribution to the common good: what makes a good city – of culture?

We are arguing, therefore, that the urban church's engagement with cities of culture can be both critical and constructive. A practical, public theology that nurtures effective discipleship in relation to the Cities of Culture debate might foster individuals' pride in their own stories and experiences as worthy of inclusion in a wider narrative of identity and aspiration. A focus on the cultural assets of a city or neighbourhood, or even a particular ethnic or religious community, can help to release and forge social capital – a means by which through shared cultural activities, common bonds can be strengthened – whether through local music, sport or an iconic building. The praxis of the urban church might also be to build up congregations to contribute actively to a cultural renaissance, by hosting cultural events or fostering the collective memory of a neighbourhood. Equally, strong social or faithful capital can be a vehicle for enabling entire communities to articulate questions about what makes a good city, give spaces and opportunities for people to tell their stories, to improve the quality of life in their area. It might speak to the wider population of the things that make us human: to celebrate our own creativity but to be wary of versions of culture that are ideological, exploitative or unsustainable.

These kinds of activities are all a part of the process of building the good city, which is always a work in progress:

> if the dominant idea of much urban regeneration is one of 'delivering a good city to the people', then faith traditions offer alternative understandings ... Cities, as human dwelling places which somehow prefigure and point to the presence of God within them, are always 'under construction', and need the active and continuing participation of all parts of the community to fulfil their potential. (CULF, 2006: 4, 1.26)

7
Good Citizens

The poor are not to be considered as objects of poverty policies, which were and still are, elaborated without their involvement ... The purpose of work proliferation is to create awareness and power in the people, so that they can become the subject of change, for the kind of society they want to live in. This process of empowering the powerless to become the subjects of change occurs mainly through helping them organise themselves to face immediate local power structures. Such conflicts and confrontations in the micro level help people become conscientised and organised to deal with major issues on a large scale. (Taylor, 1996: 88)

In our evaluation of *Faithful Cities*, we made mention of the centrality of the theme of empowerment and active citizenship. Participation and governance, or the distribution and exercise of power and decision-making, are crucial to the well-being of a city, but while politicians may pay lip-service to the values of democratic participation, little is done to involve members of a local community in the processes of regeneration. The churches cannot claim to be much better in terms of empowerment, however. Little credence is given to enabling laity to understand the theological significance of their vocation. Church leaders give scant attention to the need to equip the laity to exercise their everyday faithfulness or to connect the words and actions of the liturgies in which they take part on a Sunday to the rest of their week. Much of urban church life is still cloistered in what Gibson Winter called the 'suburban captivity' of a domesticated and privatised agenda, while the urban church needs to be supported to resist both the privatisation of public space by market economics and a temptation to escape its public vocation to become a 'macrocosm of the family' (Briggs, 2004: 16). Part of what we are arguing for in this book is a theology that encourages urban congregations to put their theology into practice, but that requires a greater seriousness towards mobilising communities of faith to enable them to bring the resources of faith to bear on the pressures of daily living. It is this imperative, of urban churches and urban communities committed to 'bottom-up' empowerment, in the spirit of *Faithful Cities'* call to recognise the theological import of not only a politicised church but a democratised theology (CULF, 2006: 14–15), that motivates this chapter.

The election of Barack Obama as President of the United States has put a former broad-based organiser from Chicago into the White House. Obama's early work as a community organiser still proves influential in shaping his vision of politics and the style of his rhetoric (Klein, 2008). Citizens' organising, which has played a significant part in the churches' involvement in community empowerment throughout the world, has suddenly achieved unexpected respectability in the UK. Originating in Chicago in the 1940s, broad-based organising has been slow to translate into the UK context, although it was in January 1996 that Stephen was able to begin a journey to discover further its potential for the urban church and wider communities, thanks to a fellowship given by the Barrow and Geraldine Cadbury Trust. What he discovered – not least the theological power and substance of broad-based organising's methods – led him to believe that it represents a significant contribution to a genuinely participatory approach to urban life and faith.

'Community organising' can be defined as grass-roots organising designed to mobilise communities in furtherance of their own democratic self-interest; of 'capacity-building' in the interests of citizen empowerment. Community organising emerged in Chicago in the 1930s during the Depression and was influenced by the observational, ethnographic approach of the Chicago School, studying the causes of juvenile delinquency. Saul Alinsky (1909–72), a young activist, came to believe that poverty and marginalisation lay at the roots of anti-social behaviour, and pioneered a new form of grass-roots organising promoted as an alternative to big business and corporate labour organisations. Alinsky founded the Industrial Areas Foundation in 1940 as an alliance of trades unions, ethnic minority groups, neighbourhood organisations and the churches, especially Roman Catholic parishes. Another name for community organising is often 'broad-based organising', reflecting its stress on bringing diverse groups together on the basis of a shared strategic goal.

Alinsky argued that the 'liberal' model of government (local or national), ceding power and benefits to the electorate, maintains the power differential between the political class and everyone else. He was sceptical of the ability of large corporate organisations – government, business, even trade unions – to deliver effective decisions to the people via 'trickle-down' means. 'The Prince was written [by Machiavelli] for the Haves on how to hold power. *Rules for Radicals* is written for the Have-nots on how to take it away' (Alinsky, 1989: 3). Power was never to be given away from the 'top down'; far more effective is the mobilisation of 'bottom-up' organisations working for social justice, encouragement of political literacy among ordinary people and harnessing people's innate capabilities into movements of networking, education and campaigning.

In the 1960s in the United States, methods of community organising were used extensively in the other marginalised groups. Among those inspired by Alinskian methods in community organising are Hillary Clinton and Barack Obama.

After Alinsky's death, his successor at the IAF, Ed Chambers, shifted its emphasis towards congregation-based organising, in New York and Chicago (it is still strong in many inner-city Roman Catholic parishes in Chicago). IAF had always put stress on leadership training, but Chambers developed styles that cultivated leaders' and participants' values and motivations, through a method called 'one-on-ones'. In the USA, congregational citizens' organising remains a major thread of community organising.

Broad-based organising is often seen as more confrontational than other methods of community development, in that it is suspicious of collaboration or partnership with government or enterprise (such as in programmes of neighbourhood renewal). It favours direct action, such as shareholders' boycotts of corporations, or demonstrations and strikes. (TELCO, or London Citizens, adopted Alinskian methods to gain a minimum wage for cleaners at Canary Wharf – see CULF, 2006: 71.) Essentially, citizens' organising rests on a belief in the power of 'civil society': the arena of associations, networks, social movements and citizen participation that is neither the market nor the state. It believes both in the capacity of individuals and communities to effect change; and its primary strategy is to foster and maximise the social capital of marginalised communities to enable them to take charge of their own destinies.

Many social thinkers (as well as political activists) believe that a vibrant civil society is the bedrock of a healthy democracy, because participation in civil society fosters social bonds, enhances civic skills and inspires altruistic values. Obama's watchwords, 'Yes we can! Change we can!' expresses this belief: that effective citizens are the wellspring of society (and of what makes a 'good city'). People need the resources and skills (back to 'social capital') to become empowered and active citizens, and community organising is one way of achieving that.

> Organising begins with the premise that (1) the problems facing inner-city communities do not result from a lack of effective solutions, but from a lack of power to implement these solutions; (2) that the only way for communities to build long-term power is by organising people and money around a common vision; and (3) that a viable organization can only be achieved if a broadly based indigenous leadership – and not one or two charismatic leaders – can knit together the diverse interests of their local institutions. (Obama, 1990: 38)

Writing in 1990, Obama sees the main challenge for disadvantaged urban (predominantly African American) communities as transforming political strategies from protest and civil rights (winning basic democratic rights) to longer-term strategies for taking power and using it effectively. There is a pressing need for economic participation as well as democratic rights. The election of African American and ethnic representatives may not be a panacea if they are co-opted or if it means government concedes limited ground; or if economic regeneration simply results in 'gentrification' of some areas at the expense of widespread economic improvement, migration of middle classes to suburbs. The challenges facing marginalised communities are deep-seated and need wholescale mobilisation by the people, for the people. That is, for him, why broad-based organising is so effective.

In Obama's discussion of the transformative potential of broad-based organising for empowerment we can hear echoes of Alinsky's grass-roots philosophy. Obama talks of the need to build on the capacity of local community and its reserves of 'social capital' – alliances of

> churches, block clubs [residents' associations], parent groups and any other institutions ... to pay dues, hire organizers, conduct research, develop leadership, hold rallies and education campaigns ... Once such a vehicle is formed, it holds the power to make politicians, agencies and corporations more responsive to community needs. Equally important, it enables people to break their crippling isolation from each other, to reshape their mutual values ... and rediscover the possibilities of acting collaboratively. (Obama, 1990: 2)

This is echoed by other current research into faith-based organisations in Chicago, which sees them as significant bearers of a collective, co-operative culture amidst the growing individualism and privatisation of society: 'while different congregations and groups foster different and sometimes conflicting values, their social accountability and the authority they attribute to their respective traditions contrast markedly with the individual moral autonomy sustained by the secular culture' (Livezey, 2000: 23).

In the UK, Community/citizens' organising is strongest in London, Bristol and Liverpool – see for example London Citizens, which presents itself as an alliance of the IAF, the Contextual Theology Centre of East London, the Islamic Foundation and Asylum Support networks (http://www.cof.org.uk/, accessed 09/11/08). Church Action on Poverty has also used community organising methods since 1990 in its 'Poverty Hearings'.

Stephen's encounter with broad-based organising in 1996 was part of an initiative that saw several leading urban clergy from the UK travelling to San Antonio in Texas to undertake the national training organised by the Industrial Areas Foundation, the inheritors of the Alinsky torch. The Church Urban Fund was then persuaded to make their largest ever grants to support the development of broad-based organisations in Merseyside, the Black Country, Bristol and Sheffield. The Citizens Organising foundation was set up. Organising was arriving in the UK with the support of the Industrial Areas Foundation and the sponsorship of the Barrow and Geraldine Cadbury Trust, and it seemed as if empowerment, one of the unanswered agendas from *Faith in the City*, might now be addressed.

Twelve years later, none of those organisations continue to have any substantial existence. The work of the Citizens' Organising Foundation is now focused in London with London Citizens and a rather frail organisation in Birmingham. Church Action on Poverty made a successful bid to the Government's Capacity Builders Fund and is working with IAF's rival organisation, the Gamaliel Foundation, to set up new organisations in Manchester, Bradford and Middlesborough.

It has been a long and difficult road. Some of the story is affected by the way power is distributed in the UK. Local democracy is much weaker than the United States and power much more centralised. The faith communities have far lower membership levels, with only the Muslim and Roman Catholic congregations having the sort of numbers that organisers need to deliver to their assemblies. The Church of England has also been equivocal about its support at senior levels. David Sheppard and Derek Worlock were used to having direct access to ministers and council leaders in Liverpool, when the Merseyside broad-based organisation was being established. The notion that their undoubtedly benign power should be subservient to this sort of organisation presented problems for them. Other church leaders have struggled with Organising's views towards power and conflict. 'Big' Ed Chambers, the national lead organiser of the Industrial Areas Foundation writes as follows:

> Power is a loaded word. Those who call themselves realists take it for granted and try to use it shrewdly in pursuing their agendas. Idealists are prone to see power as negative if not downright evil, as something to be avoided. A cardinal archbishop once said to me, 'I have trouble with the word "power"; I call it truth.' He didn't understand that power has a Trinitarian character; I and you create a 'we the people', a new reality. Beyond minimal forms like voting or jury duty, ordinary people have little direct experience of exercising power in public life. Power is the ability to act. Like the capacity to love, it is given to us at birth. Power is our birthright, our inheritance. It is the basis of our capacity to address differences through politics. (Chambers, 2004: 27).

The discovery and use of 'self-interest' in polarity with self-sacrifice also raises considerable unease among some Christians. Organising has at its heart the 'one-on-one' encounter – a relational meeting designed to discover what really matters to people, what are the spirit and values of the other. It is a listening meeting, about developing what Chambers calls a 'public relationship' (2004: 52ff.). It is there to unlock the *collective* potential of an individual's self-interest (Livezey, 2000: 14).

> Self-interest is the natural concern of a creature for its survival and well-being. It's the fundamental priority underlying the choices we make. Self-interest is based on nature's mandate that we secure the basic needs and necessities of life and develops further to include more complex desires and requirements. Healthy self-interest is one of the marks of integrity and wholeness in a person. It is the source of the initiative, creativity and drive of human beings who are fully alive. (Chambers, 2004: 52)

There needs to be a clear distinction between the 'one-on-one' meeting and the traditional relationships of pastoral care. It is also not about making friendships. Learning what is important, what matters to people, what is in their self-interest is not something that comes easily to the natural British reserve. On first encounter we do not tend to give away much of what makes us tick, perhaps in contrast to the more outgoing American personality. Seeing the charismatic American organiser Ernie Cortes having a one-on-one done on him by the lead organiser in Austin, Texas, followed by evaluation, was a fascinating experience. This model has much to teach those responsible for clergy training on the importance of relationships to the health of any community, on how to give meaning to the way in which we encounter people and begin to build an organisation which can certainly be a church. In an inversion of the feminist slogan of the 1970s, for community organising the 'political' is always also 'personal'. It is also interesting to reflect that while we are encouraged to see the basis of church life as grounded relationships of love, fellowship and mutual care, so much of the interaction within congregations is inconsequential and superficial, and the dynamic between clergy and laity one of patho-logical co-dependency. By contrast, community organising offers the basis of the bridge into a more purposeful relationship, which means two people have actually met with one another, learnt about each other and discovered something about each other's self-interest. That meeting then provides an opportunity for a decision to be made as to whether the organisation that is being represented on one side is in the self-interest of the other to join.

The church is often very unclear about the nature of the institution it is asking people to join. Is it in anybody's self-interest to sit through an hour and a quarter of Sunday worship? And yet this is the basis of all the energy and hype expended around initiatives such as 'Back to Church Sunday'! What we have to be able to offer is something that gives meaning to the whole of people's lives, at every level – spiritual, economic and social – and in their engagement with civil society. Livezey's research on religious congregations in Chicago speaks graphically of the potential of faith-based organisations in fostering resilience and collective solidarity in vulnerable communities – 'balm for Gilead' in the midst of racism, poverty and community breakdown. It illustrates how the 'moral sense' of religious traditions continues to be transmitted in and through congregational cultures, generating both intrinsic and extrinsic goods – what Livezey terms respectively, 'member benefits' and 'public benefits' (Livezey, 2000: 20). It is a perfect example of how urban religion delivers 'bonding', 'bridging' and 'linking' social capital:

> religious institutions made up of people of every color and creed that invite their members to get acquainted with one another, provide safe havens for members' (and neighbors') children, promote family values, facilitate homeownership, attempt to channel behavior in constructive directions and discourage indulgence in temptations, promote concern for others who themselves are expected to hew to the standards of the group, nurture positive identifications when negative ones are so near at hand, offer moral support and a psychological shield against a perceivedly hostile society, and promote spiritual growth where pressures of the job are experienced as soul-deadening. (Warner, 2000: 298)

It is interesting to note that the etymological origins of words such as 'civic', 'citizen' and 'civilisation' are linked around associations not just with belonging to and inhabiting the city, but with exercising the duties that pertain properly to a citizen. It is therefore intriguing, in the context of a discussion about the nature of citizenship and participation, to come across the following definition from M. Scott Peck, who identifies 'incivility' as the misuse of power:

> An organisation is most unlikely to do the hard work of community maintenance unless it has a task above and beyond the community itself – a task so important that ongoing community is required through its accomplishment. For this reason, I am doubtful how long organisation for relatively minor tasks – support groups or church congregations, for instance – can sustain themselves in real community. Usually the task must be major and complex. (Peck, 1994)

The maintenance of community has to have a task beyond the simple survival of the institution and the institution needs to have a relevance beyond itself.

It may have been one of the failures of organising in the UK not to affirm during its early years the Judaeo-Christian principles that lie at the core of the theology of organising. Yet in the USA there are no such inhibitions about articulating the religious basis of community organising, exemplified by the Gamaliel Foundation whose slogan is 'Faith and Democracy' and who once employed Barack Obama as a community organiser:

> The philosophy of the Gamaliel Foundation is rooted in the best traditions of faith and democracy. All human beings are created equal. All should be given the greatest opportunity for achieving their fullest potential. All should participate in shaping the community in which they live. The ideal is far from realized ... The greatest advances in this country came when we broadened the diversity of those who sit at the decision making tables. (Gamaliel Foundation, 2008)

Similarly, Ed Chambers' book is a serious theological, as well as political, work and the intellectual objections to organising have not been challenged by serious theological reflection and debate. We need such a serious exploration of power by first acknowledging its reality in human affairs and its centrality for the message of the Gospel. In 1996, when Citizens Organising in the UK was in its infancy, Peter Selby published *Rescue: Jesus and Salvation Today*. In it he wrote:

> The rescue of God is always first and foremost a reassertion of God's authority over individuals and communities; and that has to mean that the message of rescue has to be understood and received with repentance by those who wield power ... When Jesus speaks of himself as the 'Good Shepherd' who lays down his life for the sheep, he does so in clear contrast with those other 'shepherds of Israel' who are to be described as thieves and bandits, hirelings and strangers, unlike the True Shepherd who 'knows his own and leads them in to pasture'. (Selby 1996: 49)

> The way of rescue therefore had to involve confrontation with the holders of power in the society, for its traditions, including its most solemn religious traditions, had become a tool in their hands, used against God's purpose. (Selby, 1996: 62)

The message is clear. The Christian cannot avoid an engagement with power but it has to be an engagement that involves empowerment rather than the naked exercise of power. It is depressing to witness the behaviour of some episcopal colleagues who on achieving a seat in the House of Lords begin to enter the delusion that they are now exercising real power. The diaconal dimension to episcopacy is subsumed into a world of privilege and access to those with political responsibilities. But all too often it is power with accountability, taking them further way from the very people they represent, thereby severing that vital link between the local (and the grass roots) and those in the seats of power. So it is no surprise that it is Anglican urban clergy without large congregations, Roman Catholics (often led by religious orders), mosques and Black churches who have found a home in organising in London. These are faith communities who experience powerlessness but whose understanding of the task of the organisation is broad enough to see the need to engage with power and self-interest. It exemplifies the building of 'linking' social capital between those on the fringes and those who wield power.

Joe Hasler, no friend of broad-based organising, calls for 'Christ centred and culturally focused congregations' (Hasler, 2006). His argument is that the church must be more attuned to the gifts of localism and context, thereby becoming more culturally sensitive; it is an argument that we share.

> My major plea is for the acknowledgment that we live in a multi-cultural nation and that we start to act as if this were true, even when these cultures are not defined through skin colour, and that we begin the analysis of the cultures we work among. My hope is that this will help us set out to shape churches that reflect the glory of God through the eyes of the cultures that they are part of, and from which their local ministry emerges. My plea is that Dioceses and their Bishops, or their equivalents, see one of their main tasks as helping theology across the boundaries of the variety of cultures making up any particular diocese. Doing this will demand actions that show we are becoming a polycentric church and are not dominated by any one culture. (Hasler, 2006: 106)

Hasler calls for the employment of 'church-shaping missionaries' who 'will find and encourage the ordination of local leaders who are grounded in the local familial networks of working class culture' (2006: 107). Yet most of our urban churches are now working in contexts that are far more socially pluralistic. There are still areas that can be defined as 'white working class', but the values and norms of these communities are increasingly questionable, imbued as they are by deep-seated racism. What is needed is an approach that draws together cross-cultural groupings around issues affecting the life of the community. What is impressive across the world, from the Philippines to Peru, from South Africa to Texas, is the way in which broad-based organising can draw together racially and socially divided communities in alliances of common self-interest. Chris Baker uses the example (borrowed from Putnam and Feldstein) of Valley Interfaith in Texas to illustrate the way in which organising has a policy of 'no permanent allies, no permanent friends'. Its networks among the poorest communities, and the voices and experiences they held, were brought together at 'accountability sessions' with the voices of those who had the power to change according to the wishes of those usually excluded (Baker, 2007: 134).

One memory of such a session in San Antonio remains vivid as a parable of empowerment. Maria was Hispanic, Roman Catholic and poor. San Antonio has large numbers of Hispanics living in appalling conditions. She had become a leader in Valley Interfaith and was on the training that the first 'English recruits' had been invited to. But Maria was also to chair one of the 'assemblies' (or accountability sessions) in a large school hall. There were 600 or so gathered and the speakers who were to be 'held accountable' included a former Mayor of San Antonio and the future secretary for Housing and Urban Development in the Clinton Administration, Henry Cisneros, and the Archbishop of San Antonio. Maria managed to keep the Mayor to his allocated time and get the commitments that were being looked for. But when the Archbishop spoke, time constraints seemed of no importance to him. She warned him once that his time was up. Then: 'Archbishop will you please finish and sit down.' And he did, accepting the authority of a powerless member of the laity. Later she admitted her fear, but also her enormous sense of achievement, of which she was rightly proud.

It seems then that community empowerment, which *Faith in the City* neglected, has at least found some strength around the world through the use of the Alinsky organising model. But the whole world of community development has had millions of pounds thrown at it in the last 20 years with the churches playing a significant role. Community development workers on three-year contracts funded partly by the Church Urban Fund have been a common feature of the urban landscape. There must be some question about whether this investment has made a real difference. Margaret Ledwith expresses a fundamental dissatisfaction with traditional community development models:

> Community development has been involved in decades of action against injustice, challenging patriarchal, racist and heterosexist traditions that erode human rights and undermine democracy. This has involved campaigns against violence towards women and children, against poverty, against the corporate degradation of the environment, against homophobia, racism and sexism, against deportation of asylum seekers and much more. At the same time practice has focused on the development of cooperative, local economies, healthy convivial communities, educational equity and employment opportunities.
>
> This has not been enough. We have allowed theory and practice to become dislocated from each other, rendering us vulnerable to dilution and diversion. Simultaneously, social divisions have escalated within and between countries, creating unstable societies and an unstable world. Radical community development is committed to social and environmental justice. Its vision is that of a peaceful, just and sustainable world. Its practice is critical pedagogy, which is based on a 'profound love for the world and for people' (Freire, 1996: 70). The process of liberation begins in dialogue, a critical encounter that enables people to speak their word and name their world. Freire was clear that to speak a true word is to transform the world (Freire, 1996: 68) ... Transformative change cannot be achieved without a constant preoccupation with action and reflection. (Ledwith, 2005: 171)

Ledwith sees organising as one model that expresses these ideals. What is most striking is the convergence of ideas of those coming from a Christian visionary ideal and writers such as Ledwith and Leonie Sandercock. A vision of the Kingdom is central to Jesus' teaching and to the Christian motivated to work for that Kingdom. The work of Leonie Sandercock is full of uplifting references to hope, vision and human potential that belie her stated agnosticism and that would do justice to any urban theologian or inspirational politician. We have seen already how she professes particular virtues at the heart of her vision of the good city: 'respect, caring, neighbourliness; a concern with building connections between people, building a caring human community from whatever fragile starting point;

a notion of service to others' (Sandercock, 2006: 66). What is of interest in the context of this chapter, however, is her insistence, like the philosophers of antiquity, on a form of moral discourse that has as its end the very cultivation of such virtues. Sandercock knows that this is about prioritising the pursuit of human flourishing and the things that enable the spirit to thrive within urban planning; but that this can only be sustained by a strong set of values – a faith – nurtured in the midst of struggle:

> The work of urban, social, community, environmental, and even land-use planning is fundamentally a work of hope, the work of organising hope … And this work often takes place in the face of despair … But where does this hope come from, if not from some kind of faith? (Sandercock, 2006: 65)

Community organising, too, and the vision of empowerment that it represents, may be seen as a strategy for the organisation and mobilisation of hope. While the everyday campaigns of broad-based organising may be superficially about the nitty-gritty of local politics, Sandercock points to the enduring significance of even the most mundane issues and the imperative to relate specific incidents to a wider picture of human aspiration and solidarity:

> Planning deals with people's visions for the future of their cities. What could be more precious, in terms of giving meaning to life beyond the here and now? Planning deals with land, what it means to people in the present and what they want it to mean in the future. What could be more precious, in terms of our attachments to home and place making? Planning deals with how people relate to each other within and between groups and communities. What could be more precious, in terms of our deep need for connection with others? Planning deals with how we as a community take care of one another … What could be more precious, in terms of our universal human fears of sickness, old age, poverty and death? (Sandercock, 2006: 66)

What is clear is that building the 'good city' involves changing the nature of power within the city, a process that needs to take account of everything from a change of heart to the transformation of entire structures and organisational cultures. It involves a holistic, comprehensive vision about the needs of humankind in a sustainable world. The way we do that may certainly involve us in prophetic visionary dreams. It will also involve us in negotiating new terms of engagement between rich and poor, the powerful and the dispossessed, the stranger and the long-term resident. It will involve us in a radicalism that is biblical but remains difficult for so many caught up in some of the trivia of church life or the preoccupations of 'business as usual'.

8
The Urban Church: Fit for Purpose?

Introduction

In the light of the challenges presented in previous chapters, we begin now to move towards some interim conclusions. In particular, we are concerned to give consideration to the fitness of the urban church to meet some of these challenges – which, as we have been stressing, are also opportunities: for renewing the church's commitment to a God who 'takes place' in the everyday lives and neighbourhoods of urban humanity, and for articulating new patterns of ministry and mission as a result.

Media representation of the mainstream denominations, and the Anglican Communion in particular, is one of backward, fractious and neurotic organisations, whose claims to exercise influence in public life are increasingly irrational and illegitimate. While the churches are far from perfect, our thesis has been that they are nowhere near as detached from normality as critics contend – on the contrary, the closer one gets to ground level, the more impressive and effective the local church appears.

In Chapter 5, we argued that the commitment to the local and specific carried in the DNA of the Church of England's parish system is ripe for reinvention in the shape of a 'new localism' that values space and place as the site for constructive partnership and a strong sense of identity. Working for the good of the city begins and ends in the local: but what needs to change in the life of the urban church for this to be fulfilled? What principles and strategies should guide such commitment? How can the urban church be truly fit for purpose? In this chapter, we will argue that the Church of England at local and national level needs to be adequately resourced and equipped to continue this task; and we consider how the possibilities of involvement in welfare reform return us, once more, to the necessity of a clear-sighted and theologically grounded participation.

We are very conscious that at first glance our work on the urban church seems to have concentrated on the Church of England and disregarded the substantial presence of many urban Pentecostal churches and independent Black-majority congregations. Yet their contribution to community life in many of our inner-city areas is substantial. The Street Pastor movement in particular has been well supported by both groups of churches. Many of the Black-majority churches have developed social welfare programmes and are increasingly involved in initiatives to improve community cohesion and combat crime.[11] To their credit, police forces across the country have worked hard to develop relationships with these churches and have certainly made important strides in regaining the confidence of the elders in the Caribbean communities.

Even in Anglican terms, the arrival of many migrants in recent years from African countries has also seen the emergence of substantial ethnic African congregations, many of them worshipping in Anglican buildings and developing relationships with existing congregations. Similar congregations of Christians (some Anglican) from the Indian subcontinent are also a feature of urban church life. It is interesting how diocesan authorities struggle to 'deal with' Marathi and Tamil congregations who clearly regard themselves as Anglican but worship in their native language! The Lambeth Conference brought home to the English bishops attending the true worldwide and ethnically diverse nature of the Anglican Communion, but when the diversity is on the English doorstep it becomes more difficult to manage.

After Lambeth

How far do the debates in the worldwide Anglican Communion match the priorities of the urban church? The Lambeth Conference of 2008 may have succeeded in avoiding schism, but unfortunately it also avoided addressing what Mike Davis calls the Urban Climateric:

> In 1950 there were 86 cities in the world with a population of more than a million; today there are 400, and by 2015 there will be at least 550. Cities have absorbed nearly two-thirds of the global population

explosion since 1950 and are currently growing by a million babies and migrants each week ... The global countryside, meanwhile, has reached its maximum population and will begin to shrink after 2020. As a result, cities will account for virtually all future world population growth, which is expected to peak in 2050. (David, 2006: 1–2)

This echoes the conclusions of the UN-HABITAT Report for 2008, which affirms that urbanisation must be considered a truly global phenomenon (2008: x). The fastest-growing cities are now in the Two-Thirds World, which interestingly mirrors the shift away from the developed world to the global South as the heartland of Christianity. Yet this convergence of trends seems not to have impinged on many of those present at Lambeth 2008. As a preparatory document produced for the Conference by the Anglican Urban Network admitted, 'We are aware that there is not a consistent understanding of urban mission issues across the provinces' (AUN, 2008: 4). Yet the paper stressed the prominence of cities as going beyond their economic or demographic impact to be crucial sites of humanity's very self-understanding:

> The city can be a place of struggle and opportunity where one might grasp a glimpse of community, of homeliness, of new ways of doing things, of change – of the kingdom – 'on earth as it is in heaven'. God is encountered, not brought into those strata of lived urban form, as human flourishing is negotiated through layers of economics, culture, religion and identity. (AUN, 2008: 1–2)

In fact, there is an increasing volume of vibrant urban theology emerging from the global South;[12] but urban concerns were strangely marginal to the proceedings at Lambeth. It seemed as if many African bishops were clinging on to the rural model of church life, seeing the village with its church, headman and ordered life as where they were experiencing church growth at the moment. Mission to the growing slums of Nairobi, Johannesburg, Windhoek and Dar-es-Salaam did not seem a priority, and many of those involved with urban mission in the global South were content to work with modest gathered congregations in minority Christian contexts.

The urban church is therefore still swimming against the stream in terms of convincing others of its gifts and needs. At a national level, there is all too often a comparable indifference to be found in the House of Bishops as that among the Lambeth primates. On visits to all the English dioceses, time and again Stephen has heard the assertion, 'We're a rural diocese.' When 80% of the population of this country lives in settlements of over 10,000 people, however, that is difficult to believe. What is really being said is that the diocese is made up of large tracts of agricultural land and a substantial number of small rural parishes which dominate the diocese's self-perception and its mission strategy. The fact that the vast majority of the population of all English dioceses live in urban communities seems to go unnoticed. From Hereford to Peterborough, from Carlisle to Truro, the way in which our urban communities flourish or fail is of vital importance. At a national, as much as a global, level it is a lesson in understanding how God is at work in a changing world.

It is clear, however, that the case for urban mission must be made anew to each generation. Stephen's fellow bishops from other parts of the Anglican Communion wonder why the English denominations are not simply following congregational growth, since their commitment to the urban appears to defy all logic. Indeed, if the Church of England, in particular, had not had its parish system reinforced by Establishment then the inner cities, outer estates and many rural communities would long ago have been abandoned to be replaced by gathered, suburban churches serving the comfortable with a comfortable gospel. This has become the predominant pattern for both the Roman Catholic and Free Churches. There are notable exceptions. The United Reformed Church has shown enormous courage with its programme of community-based ministry. Methodism has tried some exciting pieces of city-centre ministry from some of its Central Halls. The fact remains that in our inner cities and outer estates the Church of England has become the only mainstream denomination to maintain a presence in every community. Its view is that residents regardless of their faith or lack of it are parishioners with rights in relation to their parish church, and the parish priest is given responsibility to share with the diocesan bishop 'the cure of souls the care of all God's people' in his or her parish. As Elaine has argued in the past, however, such a deployment of resources against the grain may be a legacy of Establishment (Graham, 1996), but it cannot be left to chance any longer. The urban church must be prepared to argue for the gospel and missionary significance of our cities; it must be adequately resourced and trained; and it must have a clear vision of how (and why) it collaborates with other participants in the urban drama. These issues will preoccupy us for the rest of the chapter.

Resourcing the urban church

The system which keeps the Church of England in the cities is currently sustained by two important elements. The church's Established status provides a framework in English law that prevents the church from moving towards congregationalism. It is also supported by a fund of over £5.5 billion held by the Church Commissioners whose trust deed requires them to pay particular regard 'to making additional provision for the cure of souls in parishes where such assistance is most required'. In fact their funds come from two main sources: Queen Anne's Bounty, which was given to the church to help relieve poverty amongst poor clergy, and the Ecclesiastical Commissioners. The latter took much of the land and wealth of the bishops and the cathedrals in return for the financial support of the bishops and the dean and two residentary canons in each cathedral. The 43 mainland dioceses also took over parish glebe land and property, giving many of them substantial financial reserves. These are obviously extraordinarily varied amounts, with dioceses like Lincoln, London and Oxford sitting on enormous financial reserves, while Durham, Newcastle and Sheffield struggle to survive. It is no coincidence that Lincoln has one of the lowest per capita giving levels nationally while Sheffield one of the highest.

Each year the Church Commissioners make an allocation of money to the Archbishops' Council. There is comparatively little room for manoeuvre as to how this is spent as the around £25 million is allocated to the neediest dioceses. There is a complicated formula, sometimes hotly contested, which ensures that most goes to dioceses with few historic resources, large populations and areas of social deprivation and poverty. Without this money, many of the northern dioceses would have to withdraw completely from the poorer urban parishes, and even a diocese like Chelmsford would find it hard to sustain much of its work in the East End of London.

In recent years the Church Commissioners have been extraordinarily well led by two First Estates Commissioners who are ultimately responsible for managing the investments. Sir Michael Colman and Andreas Whittam-Smith turned a badly damaged institution into one of the most successfully managed investment funds in the country. Despite the fact that they were rightly charged with an ethical investment policy, the Commissioners helped the church survive a major crisis over pensions and provided some additional funds for parish mission, the Church Urban Fund and money for mission initiatives in areas of housing growth or major regeneration. The percentage of diocesan finance that came from the Commissioners has dropped dramatically over the years, but parish giving has increased enormously. Nevertheless, some dioceses are able to believe themselves to be self-sufficient.

It is nonetheless a continual struggle to bring any sense of financial reality to many in the church and to reach an equitable balance between competing demands. One earlier First Estates Commissioner used to remind the General Synod that there is 'only one pot of money' in the Church of England. The money paid by the Archbishops' Council and Church Commissioners is money taken away from the dioceses and the poorer parishes, not extracted from some bottomless central bank. The result of that is that decisions have to be made. If the church spends excessively on bishops and their houses there is going to be less in the way of cross-subsidisation and selective allocations to the dioceses, and thus the money demanded from poorer parishes will be greater. It is they who are paying to maintain Auckland Castle for the Bishop of Durham and Rose Castle for the Bishop of Carlisle. It is therefore not difficult to conclude that it is the poor dioceses and parishes that will end up paying for the deficit on the Lambeth Conference.

Members of the Board of Governors of the Church Commissioners have struggled with these realities over the years, and yet our parish system and its national coverage is one of the great glories of the Church of England – and integral, we contend, to its missionary strategy. Both *Faith in the City* and *Faithful Cities* recommended, for sound theological reasons, that the church stayed in the city and resourced that process. Despite financial subsidy from the Commissioners, however, the decline in the number of stipendiary clergy is already leading to the closure of a large number of inner-city and outer-estate churches, with the remaining clergy being asked to take on more than one parish with populations of well over 12,000. A neighbouring suburban parish with a population of half that number and with several non-stipendiary lay and ordained ministers will not be asked for similar sacrifices if it is paying a parish share of more than £30,000. It becomes 'viable' in the eyes of archidiaconal and episcopal decision-makers. What spirit of mutual accountability between rich and poor does this represent?

There is a very real danger that the Church of England might begin to replicate the growth in inequalities that we are seeing in our nation. *Faith in the City* noted that per capita giving was proportionately higher in Urban Priority Areas, a characteristic that continues in many dioceses to this day. In Manchester Diocese, per capita giving in Moss Side is much higher than in the leafier parts of Bolton. The problem is that financial giving is not underpinned by any sense of mutuality or redistribution between fellow members of the Body of Christ, so articulate church members from successful suburban parishes believe this entitles them to be self-sufficient and to perceive their parish share as a form of 'taxation' which they do their best to avoid. Meanwhile, the urban deaneries almost universally find 100% of their quotas year after year, and yet many have seen serious depopulation as regeneration programmes have begun to have a major impact. During these periods there is an argument for a greater deployment of resources so that the church is seen to be active at the heart of the regeneration process, helping to shape the future communities. Fortunately, across the country there are some very able priests who have done exactly that, but almost universally there is a complaint of a lack of understanding and support from diocesan and episcopal structures.

Financial considerations must be accompanied by moral support. Sadly, comparatively few church leaders have worked and ministered in urban areas. Those who have make a very real difference on the evidence of listening to hundreds of 'frontline' urban clergy. They will spend time listening, looking and praying with those clergy ensuring that those extra acts of kindness and appreciation that mean so much are part of their pattern of support. Every bishop needs to ensure that as part of his episcopal team there is a priest with a real understanding of the demands and stresses of urban ministry to whom he will listen and seek advice. One of the most significant pieces of work Stephen undertook during his time as Bishop for Urban Life and Faith was the Urban Clergy Consultations. Over 150 clergy nominated by the bishops as working in some of the most demanding urban contexts were brought together for three days in comfortable surroundings to feel valued, listened to and encouraged. The responses were universally moving. Clergy felt able to tell their stories in a confidential and supportive environment, and the very process of the storytelling was theologically and spiritually uplifting. If the urban church is to survive and the parish system to be effective, there must be advocates for the poor and powerless in diocesan politics who will be listened to and who can influence decisions around deployment and finance. There must also be proper resources available for the support of clergy working in communities 'on the edge'.

Taking place: the role of church buildings

Harvey Cox's iconoclastic vision of the secular city, in which the urban church is called to dissolve its own structures and sacred places in order to fulfil the callings of humanity come of age, now seems somewhat anachronistic. Nevertheless, that highly kenotic and non-institutional sentiment is still in evidence when Christians say things like, 'the church is not a building, but the people'. This is, of course, an important truth; and yet in another way, our research into the future of the urban church leads us to argue that it often underestimates the resources it can offer to the wider community in the shape of its buildings and physical plant. As icons of the sacred, as places of hospitality, as centres of capacity-building, these are not inconsequential in equipping the church for its mission and ministry. A number of case studies will serve as illustration.

In December 2008 the Archdeacon of Birmingham announced that the Church of St Philip and St James, Hodge Hill, was unsafe, had been closed and was to be demolished. Forty years earlier, the same church had been hailed as one of the most significant developments in post-war church architecture. It had been designed with the help of Birmingham University's Institute for the Study of Worship and Religious Architecture, where Professor J. G. Davies, Dr Gilbert Cope, Archdeacon Peter Bridges (a qualified architect) and Dr Martin Purdy were the significant players. Gordon Davies had made some radical written contributions to the debate about the use of church buildings in his books, *The Secular Use of Church Buildings* (1968), *Every Day God: Encountering the Holy in the World and Worship* (1973). These were the forerunners of Richard Giles and his work at St Thomas, Huddersfield, reflected in his book *Re-Pitching the Tent* (1996).

It marked a new theological approach. God was not to be locked away in the sanctuary – a holy of holies. This was an incarnational approach to architecture. God is in the midst of God's people and worship should take place in the same space as weekday activity. So in Hodge Hill, the luncheon club and senior citizens activity, the pre-school playgroup and uniformed organisations met in a church designed without division around the altar and sanctuary. The 'church' was not put away behind a screen during the week – to be revealed on Sundays – but the total activity of the church, including worship, took place in the same physical space. Nothing was too secular to be shut out, and Dennis Ede, the incumbent (and later Archdeacon of Stoke), was passionate about the model. People's conservatism was quickly overcome and forty years later the Archdeacon was still remarking on the wide range of weekday activity and the good congregational life of a parish serving one of the needier estates in Birmingham. By 2008, however, £250,000 was needed for repair. The promised new church building will probably cost in excess of £1 million. In the history of urban church life in this country, perhaps Hodge Hill deserved better treatment than simply to be pulled down, given its ground-breaking significance for approaches to church building over a period of 40 years.

St Michael's, Gospel Lane in Birmingham was opened on another large council estate in 1971. This was one of the first Anglican–Methodist partnerships and was another bold building statement. The church was used for dances and dinners although movable screens could separate off the worship space from the rest of the building. Davies' incarnational architecture was still a very difficult pill for congregations to swallow in the planning stage, so the development of a 'movawall' provided some sort of compromise. Congregations were being reminded of the ancient parish church's role as the main meeting place of every community and how the supposedly 'traditional' pew was largely a Victorian means of seating the congregations in the churches newly built for large urban conurbations. The church buildings became 'fixed' holy places and the division between sacred and secular became embedded in church life. However, as a rule pews have not been introduced to new church buildings: Coventry Cathedral was rebuilt without them and the linked chairs used there were also to be used in St Michael's, Gospel Lane, giving the opportunity to 'clear the decks' and have a dance when it was needed.

Gordon Davies also provided some of the initial inspiration for the redevelopment of St Bartholomew's, East Ham, in the mid-1970s where Martin Purdy became the architect. East Ham was undergoing enormous social and economic change and the late Victorian church seated over a thousand (uncomfortably but with plenty of space for more!), while the average Sunday congregation numbered around sixty. Heating the build-ing (to take ambient temperature up to around 55 degrees F) cost more than the average Sunday collection, but here was a building that just could not be abandoned due to its geographical location. It was at the heart of the new Borough of Newham's life, a hundred yards from the town hall, police station, technical college and shopping centre.

Feasibility studies of the kind that Purdy pioneered were in their infancy. *Faith in the City*, with its emphasis on community access and social audit, was not yet published. Purdy insisted on such an audit. The community's needs and resources were to be mapped and a vision for the future of the church in East Ham was to be developed before a line was drawn on an architectural drawing board. Such a feasibility study was produced and Purdy worked with the congregation of St Bart's using his academic and teaching background to dream dreams and raise the vision. Partnerships were developing with an expanding Christian housing association, called Springboard, working in Essex and the East End. The local authority's social services department was seeking new ways of developing initiatives with the health authority known as 'Joint Financing'. There was a need for day-care facilities for the elderly and a daily luncheon club. A medical practice was seeking a new surgery and the community needed new meeting places. There was already an active Asian women's language and social work project going on in the listed old rectory at the rear of the church, together with substantial pre-school children's activity.

The design ultimately included 27 flats in a sheltered scheme for the elderly, day-care facilities with a substantial catering kitchen, several meeting rooms, a coffee bar in an attractive lounge/foyer open all day every day and a surgery complex for four doctors, built as an investment by the diocese out of glebe funds. The old rectory ultimately provided additional flats and a new day nursery and Asian Women's training facility. The Queen opened the complex in 1983 and 25 years later it still thrives, very much at the heart of East Ham's life. It cost £1.75 million then but became part of a major church redevelopment programme in Newham where Aston Charities, Springboard, Newham Community Renewal Programme, Mansfield House, West Ham Central Baptist Mission and the Church of England spent millions transforming the church's physical presence in the borough.

A year later Andrew Mawson arrived down the Commercial Road as the new URC minister in Bromley-by-Bow. Twenty-five years later, *Lord* Mawson's work in creating a lively social enterprise centre has been widely recognised by government and the media. Once more, at the heart of his approach has been the incarnational theology that sees the church building as a resource for the whole community. His book, *The Social Entrepreneur: Making Communities Work* (2008), has raised the profile of the church's potential for involvement in social enterprise, which paved the way for the Church of England's *Moral But No Compass* report published in 2008. In 1990 Richard Giles completed his major reordering work on St Thomas, Huddersfield. In his book *Re-Pitching the Tent* he developed a theology similar to that which Davies had brought to practical fruition at Hodge Hill, applying it to the whole reordering of existing buildings:

> Christians are to be found worshipping in long Gothic tunnels, buried beneath heaving seas of pitch pine, cowering beneath balconies and lurking behind pillars. They use on a weekly if not daily basis buildings without running water, and with practically no heat in winter. They attempt to address God in the language of today amidst the debris of yesterday's church and the preservationist constraints imposed by those who have no understanding of the Christian vocation. They are hampered and hindered as no previous Christian generation ever was by the buildings erected to serve them but which now subdue them. If the Church maintains any desire to proclaim 'release to the captive' it is high time it repitched its tents. (Giles, 1996: 5–6)

Giles encourages a fresh approach to existing church buildings, making the case for a complete renewal of the way in which we experience sacred space within the built environment. The emphasis is on the way in which the church is used for worship but the consequent effect on how the building can be used throughout the week releases it for the sort of social outreach opportunities that Mawson and even St Bart's made clear were possible.

> It is evident that faithful communities which wait upon the Lord, which pray, and discuss and explore and dream dreams, have been able to transform their tired old buildings into places of assembly which by their beauty, simplicity and meaning heighten consciousness of God's resplendent love, and help shape the living church which they house. (Giles, 1996: 211)

There can be no doubt that money made available by dioceses and the Church Urban Fund for parishes to take a fresh look at their buildings has enabled substantial reordering in many urban churches. The casual visitor should expect respectable toilets, kitchen facilities and warmth as well as a reasonably comfortable seat. There remains a serious problem, however. The age profile of urban congregations has led to an inbuilt conservatism. The primary task, if not a desire to return to some fanciful notion of 'things as they were', is at least to hold on to things as they are. The radicalism of approach to many of our urban church buildings, which is so desperately needed, has been compromised by congregational conservatism and architects whose solutions are formulaic narthex conversions.

There is much that could be learnt from the approach of many of our cathedrals. Cathedral life is booming, and not simply in the historic architectural masterpieces. Many of our urban 'parish church' cathedrals have seen a renaissance and have renewed their roles as major foci for the spiritual and community lives of their cities. Sheffield Cathedral's £4.5 million homelessness centre is one outstanding example. Funded with the help of European, national and local government help and substantial local fundraising, the new complex is physically part of the cathedral, and, if anything, has further highlighted the need for radical reordering inside the worship space itself. The present Dean of Durham, Michael Sadgrove, was Dean of Sheffield during the first stages of the redevelopment. Its success is undoubtedly due to the partnerships he and the then Bishop of Sheffield, Jack Nicholls, forged with the civic leaders. The cathedral and the city engaged in a process of mutual rediscovery, both learning that the flourishing of the city and the cathedral can only be achieved by effective partnership. Sadgrove writes that such buildings are central to civic identity, not simply for their functional uses but also as a symbol of transcendence:

> they are not necessarily able to accommodate great crowds of people (the medieval cathedrals were not built for this purpose either). It is rather to achieve in terms of spatial and aesthetic quality a sufficient sense of the numinous that can function symbolically as both sacred and public space in their own right ... At Liverpool and Coventry, opportunity arose to create such spaces anew in a way that could invest the 'temple' with the same presence and dignity as the city's peer institutions of academy, town hall, gymnasium and market place. (Sadgrove, 2006: 96)

As our story of Halifax Parish Church illustrated in the Introduction, cathedrals and city-centre churches are often important foci for the community, as centres of civic celebration or debate. With the increasing privatisation or commercialisation of public space, there is perhaps a role for buildings as a 'forum' for the people. Such historic church buildings are not just museum pieces, therefore, but have an opportunity to recover their monastic roots as agents for social outreach, hospitality and transformation within their communities. They sit alongside the other seats of power in their cities as the Christian conscience of their communities, with a role as both prophet and deacon, or servant. The quality of the service they offer to those in need will be proportionate to their right to be prophetic. Without that prophetic role at the very heart of the city, each community will be the poorer.

Building effective leadership

We have been talking about financial resources to enable the urban church to be fit for purpose, and whether its ecclesial polity really delivers the kind of cross-subsidisation, which circumstances require and a Pauline theology of interdependence and mutuality demands. However, the urban church needs to be fit for purpose in other ways, not least in its preparation for accredited ministry.

Any notion that urban clergy are confined to one particular theological persuasion should be dispelled. There are a good number of 'Forward in Faith' parishes that have long played a significant part in urban ministry. The Anglo-Catholic social tradition is alive and well, and the 'flying bishops' have all acknowledged their commitment to its continued support. Evangelicalism has also seen something of a sea change. Jim Wallis and the Sojourner movement have had a significant theological impact on evangelical thinking in the last 25 years. In recent times Faithworks and Oasis Trust has played a major role in the UK in reviving evangelical commitment to social action and educational involvement. Steve Chalke and Malcolm Duncan have won a place in political affection as a one-stop shop for contact with the church communities. However, the departure of a charismatic leader from these non-church, non-denominational organisations often renders them vulnerable.

The Message Trust, based on an industrial estate on the edge of Wythenshawe, Manchester, has made a phenomenal impact on mission to young people in the North-West. Andy Hawthorne, its founder, will prove to have been one of the most significant Christian leaders of modern times. The Eden project, based in Manchester, where groups of young adults commit themselves to living in some of the neediest communities for a period of years, has been an undoubted success in reaching disaffected young people. An early presumption that they were arriving in communities where 'nothing was happening' produced resentment from local churches. Now Eden normally works in partnership with a local church, which could be of any denomination but is likely to be of an evangelical persuasion. Hope 08 has had a clear social and community dimension with a strong biblical understanding of injustice and poverty at the heart of its message. These sorts of initiatives have kept the social dimension of the Christian Gospel very much alive for many evangelicals, and prevented any drift towards an equivalent of the 'religious Right' in the United States of America. This is not to say that large Anglican evangelical parishes, with a strong emphasis on a biblical teaching ministry and evangelistic outreach, are not alive and well. There are influential and successful examples in every diocese, but despite their best efforts to suggest that others should imitate their 'success' they remain only one part of the rich spectrum of the Church of England parish system. Their ethos will not necessarily always meet the needs of struggling urban communities for whom the Gospel is most powerfully expressed in supportive service rather than a call to conversion.

Nevertheless, there has to be considerable concern about the lack of training and the development of clergy and lay people working in the urban context. With one or two notable exceptions, our theological colleges seem to see the development of an urban contextual theology among ordinands as an optional extra that may be remedied by a summer placement. Westcott House, Cambridge, in partnership with the Diocese of Manchester, has kept a house in Longsight, Manchester, that provides a compulsory residential term's placement for all single students. There is a part-time tutor (an experienced urban priest) who resources and oversees the project in Manchester, supported now by a very experienced group of supervisors, some of whom have been working with students for over ten years. For many the term in Manchester has proved the most significant period of their theological training. It provides an opportunity to live in a small community (a redundant vicarage), in a multi-ethnic and multi-faith parish with opportunities for sharing in urban ministry with men and women often of an entirely different theological and worship tradition. The scheme has produced some of the most able urban clergy working for the Church of England.

Newcastle Diocese started a similar project in 1999 by (now Archdeacon) Peter Robinson, then working on the Byker estate. Its vision is 'that changes taking place in the East End of Newcastle embody the kingdom of God; that new forms of church presence emerge that honour the current context; that we share our learning with those outside our situation and learn from them.'[13] Here the model has been an active involvement by the churches in the regeneration of East Newcastle from which learning and reflection can be offered to those seeking employment as clergy or lay people in the urban context. Cranmer Hall, Durham, has used UMTP as part of its ordination training programme with some success.

Other colleges have more mixed track records. Ripon College Cuddesdon recently closed down its centre on Sheffield's Manor Estate. At present this has been replaced by a 'taster day' on urban ministry at the college, in rural Oxfordshire, in the hope that students might be encouraged to take on urban ministry placements. Queen's Birmingham had a similar project in Handsworth, which has recently been revived. In partnership with the Christian solicitors' practice of Anthony Collins they are embarking on a restructuring of their urban ministry training. The Nehemiah Project, which Anthony Collins started, works with local organisations over an 18-month period in the support and training of regeneration workers who will develop a plan for their neighbourhood and communities to enable lasting transformation. Lay and ordained workers have taken advantage of this opportunity and there is a hope that it can be offered in other areas of the country.

Most Church of England theological colleges have placement opportunities, but whereas Westcott offers both urban and rural programmes designed to develop contextual reflection, others do not seem prepared to be as radical. There is a particular problem with some of the evangelical colleges, in that many products of 'successful suburban' parishes in the South East are only prepared to return to serve their titles in such parishes. They have much to learn from the pioneering work done at the College of the Nazarene in Manchester, a traditional Bible College, now transformed into a lively institution determined to offer relevant training for ministers working in the urban context. Similarly, the newly established Southern North-West Training Partnership has benefited from the work done at

Luther King House in Manchester by the Methodists, United Reformed Church and the Baptists in developing a contextual learning model for ministerial training. This includes a long-standing and pioneering programme for training church-related community workers (Ballard and Husselbee, 2008). However, while Nonconformist denominations have blazed a trail in patterns of training for lay and contextual ministry, the establishment of the new Regional Training Partnerships must not be allowed to result in a drift of resources away from lay adult education.

Sheffield's long-established Urban Theology Unit, founded by the charismatic urban prophet John Vincent, still offers an impressive programme of urban training at both undergraduate and postgraduate level. Its library has one of the finest collections of urban theological resources in the United Kingdom and there are many distinguished urban practitioners who have benefited from the UTU experience. Now linked with York St John University, it declares a commitment to:

> the radical Gospel of the Kingdom, the search for Christian discipleship and vocation in the city, the empowerment of the poor and powerless, the theological and ministerial potential of each Christian, the specific context in which theology, ministry and action take place, the participation of people in their own education and liberation. Through its structure and work UTU will promote theological and biblical reflection on the realities of the church in the urban context of modern Britain, encourage styles, strategies and spiritualities which are effective for mission in an urban setting, facilitate the emergence of new or alternative forms of church life more appropriate to the marginalized peoples of modern Britain, generate Gospel projects relevant to a particular situation, foster vocation to inner city ministry and discipleship, challenge complacent and comfortable forms of modern Christianity which ignore the poor, affirm the role and significance of powerless members of society and support those who, in the light of the Kingdom, are dissatisfied with the world, the church and their structures and seek to change them. (Mission Statement on http://www.utusheffield.org.uk)

This has the ring of an exciting urban political manifesto for the church and the urban Christian (ordained and lay), which no doubt deters many of the conservative institutions it seeks to influence and change. Somehow the tremendous resource that is UTU has to be captured more effectively for ministerial and lay training by the urban church. This should not be regarded as specialist training for those 'who like that sort of thing', but a valuable opportunity for learning for anyone, regardless of their particular context.

We reiterate, however: such urban, contextually based training must go beyond a statutory summer placement or token urban seminar, and should expand its horizons to consider how effective training might be offered to those in secular employment, as policy-makers, public servants and community workers, as well as clergy. When we visited Chicago in August 2004, we were highly impressed by the work of the Seminary Consortium for Urban Pastoral Education (SCUPE). Founded in 1974, SCUPE has its roots in Reformed evangelical seminaries in the Mid-West, but now sponsors a Master's programme in community development for local faith-based activists in partnership with a local public college, North Park University. SCUPE also runs a programme called the 'Chicago Semester', which works with a broad range of undergraduate students regardless of their chosen subject specialism. Chicago Semester is more than a one-off 'urban placement', and seeks to foster in many types of Christian young people a sense of vocation that is explicitly theologically driven but not necessarily directed exclusively towards ordination. The directors of Chicago Semester stress the value of their programme in fostering a sense of public service in their participants: a sense of vocation that goes beyond the individual calling, to embrace a more comprehensive understanding of the 'common good'. Moreover, in its emphasis on experiential learning and theological reflection on practice, the scheme represents a very innovative and exciting pattern of formation.

How does the Church of England resource the network of urban mission that can be found in every urban community? At diocesan level support is patchy. A few have urban officers, usually part-time and sometimes combining a generalist role with the specific work of supporting Church Urban Fund applications from the diocese. Nationally, the Bishop for Urban Life and Faith and the Mission and Public Affairs' Secretary for Urban Affairs have called representatives of the diocesan bishops together twice a year. Initially this was to monitor progress on the implementation of *Faithful Cities*, but it has also provided a forum for debate with government and exchange of good practice and experience. A network of this kind has to be sustained and encouraged at both national and diocesan level if clergy and lay workers are not to feel isolated from others facing similar challenges.

The Urban Bishops' panel of the House of Bishops predated *Faith in the City* and has been in existence for over twenty-five years. Initially it was a support group of diocesan bishops facing the challenges of Thatcher's urban Britain. It later became an official panel or sub-committee of the House of Bishops, along with similar arrangements for the rural bishops. Potentially it has considerable strategic importance politically, both within the church and beyond, but it is weakened by poor attendance. It could serve as a point of interaction between urban bishops, church and state. As ever within the Church of England, however, the recognition that the diocese is the primary unit of mission weakens the ability of the church nationally to deliver coherent policy thinking and prevents bishops from giving priority to strengthening the role and perception of the church in the public domain. It should also be taking a lead in encouraging urban theological learning, training and research. The commissioning of *Moral But No Compass* (see below), possible without the approval of General Synod and externally funded, could provide a template for other significant pieces of research and theological reflection on issues that are challenging for the urban church.

Church Urban Fund

The Church Urban Fund is one of the Church of England's great success stories of the last 20 years. Launched after the publication of *Faith in the City* it captured the church's imagination and conscience, the bulk of its resources being found from an appeal to the dioceses. Given targets, dioceses felt a real commitment to raise substantial sums and the fund was able to raise sufficient capital to spend over the initial 20 years of life. It transformed the perception of the church in town halls and government departments into a serious player in regeneration programmes and new projects, a partner to be courted and valued. Leverage on other funding exceeded expectations as other charitable trusts began to recognise the quality of CUF's work. It was local, well managed and monitored (although there have been some exceptions!) and it has made a real difference in local needy communities. From the beginning, the priority has been the poorest parishes from the beginning, with Z-scores being the first measure used to discover the neediest 10% of parishes in the land (ACUPA, 1985: 21, 1.42). Later, the Index of Multiple Deprivation was used with the help of the Church Commissioners to map information from the census for every English parish. This now provides a unique profile of every parish, available through geographic information mapping open to every diocese.

The church and CUF wrestled with its future, both among the trustees and at the General Synod. To let go of such an important organisation would have been a major blow to the church's credibility nationally and locally. The wealth of experience and knowledge that CUF has built up over 20 years work and thousands of projects is enormous. In the end money was found from the Commissioners/Archbishops' Council to fund a transition period while CUF built up a base of supporters and income sufficient to sustain ongoing grant-making at around £2.5 million for the foreseeable future. The trustees were able to gain funding for CUF Xchange, designed to share good practice across the country, and indications are that the campaign is going to be a success; in the meantime CUF has seen the need to rethink some of its grant-making strategy and future directions for the trust.

Decision-making for many grants has now been devolved to the large urban dioceses, with an annual grant allocation being made to them based on their own strategies. Money has been made available for relieving the worst of rural poverty (now identifiable through the Index of Multiple Deprivation at a very local level) and coastal communities have also benefited. The trustees have also renewed their sense of 'belonging' to the Church of England. Although grants have been given to almost every denomination and faith, the fact that CUF is now working from Church House, and clearly must rely on the church for the bulk of its future funding, has enabled an important debate to take place about its role as a resource for the church in its wider mission.

Whither the urban church? The future of welfare

It is into this context that the debate about the church's involvement in statutory welfare provision began to take place. CUF's work had been primarily project-led. Usually a grant would be given for an initial three years, with possible extensions to five, and in rare cases seven years. The work was to be innovative, locally managed, of benefit to the needs of the local community. Long-term funding had to be sought from other sources. Much of the work it sponsored has gone to now well-established community organisations that are still making a real difference at local level. Other work has come to an end; maybe the original needs having passed or the short-term nature of the work fulfilled. At the same time, however, both the Government and the Opposition began to talk seriously about the 'Third Sector' taking a much greater role in the provision of welfare previously provided by local or health authorities.

The Church of England had already taken up the challenge of a major increase in its involvement in secondary education with its commitment to the academies programme, which has delivered more than seventy new secondary schools. The question asked by government was therefore, 'Why shouldn't the church take on some responsibility for the care for the elderly suffering from dementia, helping the workless back to employment, providing health-care facilities or improving its delivery of services to children and families?'

The only way these questions were going to be seriously considered by the Church of England was after a serious piece of research. Thanks to the Esmee Fairburn Trust, the Diocese of Southwark and the Church and Community Fund, research was commissioned from the Von Hügel Institute at Cambridge University, which reported in May 2008. The report was sharp in its analysis, pointing to:

> The absence of an evidence base on the Church's huge moral and civic contribution – and the seeming lack of interest in even seriously considering it – has meant that the state is planning without vision or roots and not even recognising its own creed of 'what works'... We have encountered a Church that had been under the (mistaken) impression that it is well understood in Government, and a government that is highly limited in its understanding of the Church. (Davis, Paulhus and Bradstock, 2008: 95)

The report makes it clear the Church of England is the largest voluntary sector organisation in the country, with a complete national coverage and enormous expertise and experience in service delivery. It is already, at local level, engaged in some contractual service delivery, but there is a real possibility to move into this area as part of a new strategy to support the continued development of the existing Anglican contributions to health and social care, community development, post-compulsory education, criminal justice, asylum and refugee advice and services, welfare-to-work, job creation, the rural economy and the arts and cultural economy. It would also encourage increased utilisation and coordination of activities in civic hubs of cathedrals and dioceses. (Davis, Paulhus and Bradstock, 2008: 96)

While the report is reluctant to engage in sustained theological reflection, it does articulate some critical questions for the church. Is such involvement consistent with the church's self-understanding? Does the church have sufficient capacity to deliver such programmes? Is this a distraction from its core activity of mission, or part of it? Does it compromise the church's independence or ability to exercise prophetic ministry in relation to government?

The reception of the report, despite an unfortunate leak in advance by *The Times* newspaper, was fascinating. Government reaction was defensive of the report's accusation 'that when it comes to faith communities in general, and aspects of charity law and social policy in particular, the government is planning blind [sic] and failing parts of civil society ... The government has good intentions, but is moral without a compass' (Davis, Paulhus and Bradstock, 2008: 13). Publicly, ministers rejected the report's criticism, but some acknowledged privately that the Church of England's role had been seriously underplayed in the face of some rampant secularism. Faithworks' role as the 'one-stop' shop representing the Christian churches also had to come under some closer scrutiny. The initial reaction on the part of the Church of England, meanwhile, was one of welcome for the recognition of what was actually being delivered at a local level, but also the potential for future mission development. The examples of work done by Anglicans in Australia and Hong Kong and by the Lutherans in northern Europe showed what was possible. None of the governments in these countries seem to have a problem with a clear Christian identification with the service offered. Nevertheless, there remain questions about the nature of political engagement with the church. Government may regard the church as a provider of services, a good source of social capital and as made up of people with strong traditions of philanthropy and volunteering, but do they understand the transformative vision at the heart of the Christian faith? Are they prepared to allow and encourage the distinctive values of faith-based welfare provision?

The report makes the valid point that the churches' thinking also needs to catch up with the changing context of welfare. Mainstream Anglican social thought may still be caught in the shadow of William Temple's enthusiastic endorsement of the state-funded, centralised model of the Welfare State established after 1945, without considering how times have changed. Temple greeted the Beveridge report of 1942 as 'the first time anyone had set out to embody the whole spirit of the Christian ethic in an Act of Parliament', which reflects a particular theological position that regarded 'secular reason' and government bodies as capable of embodying and fulfilling the deepest values of the Kingdom. What if those institutions fall short of Christian values, however, or if there is evidence that agencies other than government might be more effective in delivering them? Can secular institutions or legislation 'embody the whole spirit of the Christian ethic', or is that the mission of the church? Such considerations point us back to the theological issues in Chapter 1, and suggest a theology of 'radical Christian Realism' in which active partnership with the state must be tempered by a critical recognition that no human political economy can deliver heaven on earth (Baker, 2007: 95–109). This public theology must therefore nurture the role of prophet, as well as servant, church:

> Prophetic statements, in addition to possibly challenging the status quo, may offer alternative visions of society. Such visions, though, will only have impact if they are grounded in a sound analysis of the social, economic and political dynamic of the situation being addressed. Some of the rhetoric we encountered in sections of the Church about government officials, members of professions, trade unions, voluntary agencies and 'the poor' being 'always virtuous', while business leaders, entrepreneurs, and public managers never can be, clearly lacks such realistic grounding. It also unreflectively avoids a deep understanding of human motivation, agency and action, let alone a nuanced theology of 'sin'. (Davis, Paulhus and Bradstock, 2008: 47)

In February 2009 the General Synod received a report from the Bishop for Urban Life and Faith about the reaction to *Moral But No Compass* (GS Misc. 912):

> Since the report was published the wider social context has been radically changed by the speed with which the British (and global

economy) has entered recession. The Government's approach to welfare delivery must now adapt to rising unemployment and lower tax receipts together with, it can be expected, increased social stress among communities that are already economically vulnerable. (Lowe, 2009: 9)

The report relates the work that has been going on with civil servants from the Department of Communities and Local Government in looking to the Church Urban Fund in partnership with Anthony Collins Solicitors to provide, with government help, support for local churches who wish to get involved in welfare provision. This will be a development of the new CUF Xchange unit and the next two years will be a test of both the Government's commitment to supporting faith participation in welfare provision and the church's ability to deliver.

Meanwhile, through a think-tank led by Ian Duncan-Smith the Conservative Party has produced a comprehensive study of the state of Britain and some potential policy ideas, entitled *Breakthrough Britain* (Centre for Social Justice, 2007). Although much mention was made, once again, of local church and Christian organisations there was no representative of mainstream churches on the working party on the Third Sector. The same confusion exists within government. The Office of the Third Sector, part of the Cabinet Office, looks after the Government's relationship with the voluntary sector. But the church is seen as part of the 'faith communities sector', located and supported by a junior minister in Communities and Local Government. As a result ministers and civil servants see their priorities focused on dealing with Islamic extremism and treating all the faith communities in an even-handed way despite relative differences in size. It is a muddle, leading to confusion within the church where archbishops can open prime ministerial doors without always linking up with the national church institutions and networks. It leads to confusion in government, where, desperate to find the one-stop shop for Christians, it works with Faithworks or relies on one-off conversations with individual bishops. There is a desperate need for a new political conversation – and what used to be called 'joined-up government' – about the place of the Church of England in relationship to government and the readiness of government to work openly with an organisation motivated by Christian vision, teaching and values.

For its part, the urban church can certainly provide the voluntary and professional personnel and practical help in such initiatives, but it must also continue to reflect theologically and strategically on the underlying principles. If Archbishop Sentamu's sentiments are to be believed (see Chapter 5), this will perform a valuable function in helping the whole community to recover its 'moral compass' as part of a national debate, and to discover how policy proposals are rooted in particular visions of what it means to be human:

> While Christians seek to draw principles for action from Scripture, preaching and tradition ('what matters'), modern governments depend on 'evidence-based policy' – an approach that claims to focus on 'what works'. However, a closer inspection of the ethics, values and principles informing many policy choices and positions suggests that they are ... rooted in a profound understanding of what constitutes human flourishing. (Davis, Paulhus and Bradstock, 2008: 49)

This applies to all policy initiatives, and indeed any arguments advanced in support of the survival of the urban church. In order to be fit for purpose, however, it must be appropriately resourced, effectively equipped and theologically inspired.

Conclusion
A Vision for the City

The walk from the Bishop's House on the Old Moat Estate in South Manchester to the newsagents is no more than 200 metres. The first house is occupied by an elderly woman who has lived there since the house and the (now demolished) church were built. She is a perfect example of someone who has given years of faithful, mainly unsung, service to her local church. Next door is a Hindu family. Every morning, as the father leaves for work and to take his children to school, he lights a candle on the shrine by his front door and quietly says a prayer. Open the newsagent's shop door and the owner has his head buried in the Qur'an, a broad-minded Muslim who seems to have no difficulty in maintaining a well-stocked 'top shelf'.

This is not the most disadvantaged estate in Manchester. The Church of England's presence, although frail, is real and has been since the estate was built, originally with a massive and imposing building, now with an adapted church hall. Council house sales have led to a more socially and ethnically mixed community, but it is still easy to identify the rented properties unadorned by the porches and leaded windows of the property-owning democracy. Despite claims to the contrary, faith is still central to many residents' lives in this community. The most popular and sought-after school in South Manchester is Trinity, a Church of England comprehensive in Moss Side. The school's aim is to provide 'a Christian environment in which young people are safe, secure, cared for and happy and are able to develop into articulate, confident and well-qualified citizens of the world'. The school is multi-ethnic, multi-faith, drawing from a wide range of socio-economic backgrounds, reflecting the communities from which it is drawn. It is a high-achieving school. Faith is not disregarded or set aside but valued and nurtured. It reflects something of the vision that we have been trying to convey for 'the good city', the need for 'articulate, confident and well-qualified citizens of the world'.

All these examples provide illustrations of what it means to have 'faith in the city' at the beginning of the twenty-first century. When the members of the Commission for Urban Priority Areas concluded their report *Faith in the City* in 1985, they ended with a tribute to those living and working in urban priority areas, whose stories had made such an impression on them:

> each of us has faced a personal challenge to our lives and life styles: a call to change our thinking and action in such a way as to help us to stand more closely alongside the risen Christ with those who are poor and powerless. We have found faith in the city. (ACUPA, 1985: 360, 15.10; see also above, p. 26)

This closing sentiment was, of course, both an expression of the Commission's deep conviction that the church must stand alongside the nation's most marginalised communities in the name of justice and 'to create a society in which benefits and burdens are shared in a more equitable way' (15.9), and also a testimony to the difference people of faith were already making to their neighbourhoods. The essence of this book, too, has been about the often unspectacular but decisive contributions that 'faith' continues to make to the lives of our cities and towns. This frequently takes place against the odds of religious decline, government reticence, media hostility and ecclesiastical conservatism, but the religious presence is undeniable. Yet we have tried to unpack what it means to have 'faith in the city' for our times, and concluded that the situation in which the contemporary urban church and others work and minister today is altogether more complex, perhaps, than that of 1985.

For a start, what we mean by 'faith' has changed considerably – or perhaps its changing contours are simply that much more apparent. 'Faith' for ACUPA meant predominantly Establishment, white Anglicanism, and as we have already argued, its view of the world, and most especially what could be achieved by a dialogue with government was profoundly shaped by that reality. While we have wanted to remain within a broad tradition of Anglican social thought, in valuing an incarnational Christianity that affirms the insights of secular reason and the needs of all members of a local community, regardless of professed belief, trying to articulate an urban public theology for such a situation requires some new thinking. As our illustrations at the beginning of this chapter indicate, 'faith' is still a present and daily reality in our cities – but it assumes an ever more diverse face. The most visible expressions of religion may be those that have arrived in our cities over the past two or three generations, originating from Africa, South Asia or Eastern Europe. 'Faith' now has many manifestations, many stories to tell, although we would contend that they share many basic values: the value of community, the irreducible value of human life and the importance of seeing beyond the superficial and materialistic dimensions of a society's aspirations towards a vision of a benevolent, just divine creator.

This is not to indulge in religious triumphalism or to deny the real differences between various faith traditions, or the considerable tensions that exist. 'Faith' is, in many urban communities, a fragile and precarious phenomenon, and many of the longer-standing organisations – especially the mainstream Christian denominations – face the real possibility of disappearing altogether over the next generation. Yet the evidence contained within this book suggests that if faith were to vanish from our cities, it would be profoundly missed. Faith-based organisations are regarded by government as repositories of valuable physical resources, such as plant, volunteer and paid labour and networks. As we outlined in Chapter 8, also, there is increasing reliance on faith groups in terms of service provision in areas such as education, care for the elderly, children's welfare and health promotion. Some of the motivation for this is because faiths are seen as particularly effective in extending the 'reach' of local services, but the agenda of that elusive category, 'social cohesion' also features heavily. This may be seen, variously, in exploiting the ability of faith-based organisations to build bridges between communities, to reach out to those traditionally excluded from mainstream services or to deliver well-motivated representatives into forms of local governance. However, the risks of co-option are real, and so we have argued that any engagement with such processes needs to be well informed and thoroughly grounded in a strategic, but above all theological, realism.

One of the virtues of faith-based involvement in their communities, we have argued, is that they bring not only abundant (if sometimes thinly stretched) resources of personnel and physical facilities, but a rich base of moral values and principles, derived from their traditions of belief. Within a Christian context, it has traditionally been the task of theology to

connect the demands of practical vocation with the resources of faith, in order to articulate a 'practical wisdom' by which authentic discipleship can be guided. The thesis of 'faithful capital' is one way of framing this essential inter-relationship between faith and action – that religious engagement is sustained by a public, historical and systematic world-view that demands that its adherents 'practise what they preach'.

We have tried to take account of the rising profile of faith in public policy by tracing growing opportunities for collaboration between faith-based organisations and government. However, there are still disparities between different faith groups in terms of their capacity to respond to such opportunities, and more work needs to be done to map out the 'manner in which minority faiths are engaged at the public table' (Dinham and Lowndes, 2009: 9). Inevitably, however, it is those that are longest established that have the most extensive structures and resources. In particular, it is difficult to escape the organisational weight of the Church of England, with its ability to combine comprehensive diocesan and national networks with a local presence in every square metre of the country. While we recognise that other traditions have different gifts and will not want to reproduce these structures, we cannot pretend that the Church of England does not possess such inherited advantages, but choose rather to think about the ways in which such a legacy, both structural and theological, can be made to work for the 'good of the city'. This is not simply a conservative rationalisation of the privileges of Establishment, therefore, but an attempt to rework the strengths of localism and an inclusive, performative theology in ways that can continue to uphold the common good.

Hence, in Chapters 1, 2 and 3 we spelled out some of the theological and intellectual planks of such a local, public theology. A call for the urban church to locate itself where 'God takes place' is not a nostalgic retreat into an exclusive sanctuary, but rather to understand the Triune God as always present in natural and built environments, in human affairs and in the spirit-filled communities that seek to be bearers of God's word through the generations. It calls the urban church, as Harvey Cox did forty years ago, to see beyond the structures of the institution and the strictures of doctrinal propositions in order to glimpse the face of Christ in all those struggling for the human, humane, sustainable city. Yet despite its flaws – its conservatism, its homophobia, sexism and racism, its timidity in the face of a radical Gospel – the Church as institution can be a beacon of hope in what is now the *post*-secular city: as bearer of memory, as guardian of inspirational public space, as advocate of the integrity of the local, qualities often expressed in the prominence of a church building at the heart of a community (see Chapter 8).

The church, however, not least the urban church, is ultimately its people, and the laity, priests and bishops all have their part to play. Yet fifty years on from Ted Wickham's vision of work-based industrial mission, which radically rethought the organisational basis of local involvement from parish-based to work-based participation – an intriguing parallel with the base communities of the progressive Roman Catholic Church in Latin America – there is still a paucity of resources to help the laity exercise an informed ministry in their secular vocations. The urban church must equip its congregations to exercise an 'everyday faithfulness' in their own contexts, caught increasingly as they are between a religiously indifferent or illiterate public sphere and the introspective, individualised, parochial (in the worst sense) patterns of church involvement. We have argued that Christian formation within the urban church might be characterised as a balance between the imperatives of 'citizenship' and 'discipleship': of living in this world, but not of the world, of balancing the inclusivity of common reason with the specific, often counter cultural, revelation that is Jesus Christ. This, too, must shape the kind of public theology promoted by the urban church, in word and deed: it must be one that is rooted in Christian accounts of what it means to live as the spirit-filled Body of Christ with an openness to a 'world come of age'. Whether it is the statements of a church body such as CULF, the public profile of a bishop for urban life and faith, the rationale for a funding application, or simply the ambitions of a local congregation for the future of its neighbourhood, such practices must be coherent in their philosophy, faithful to tradition, sensitive to context and transformational in their outcomes.

If religious and cultural pluralism is a reality for our urban communities, then the challenges of globalisation promise both to enrich and to undermine their well-being. Immigration is essential for a flexible and dynamic economy, and brings many cultural benefits, which in turn contribute to the attractiveness of city life. Yet as Chapters 4 and 5 indicated, many of the most dispossessed members of urban communities feel threatened and displaced by incomers, a reality to which government is only gradually awakening. Such alienation speaks of a dangerous level of exclusion on the part of the white working class, with attendant risks of the rise of far Right politics and a scandalous waste of talent, energy and ambition of those denied the chance to fulfil their potential. As Chapter 4 argued, housing policy exacerbates social and educational exclusion, which is further compounded by inequality of opportunity and a democratic deficit. No healthy democracy can tolerate the levels of political disengagement evident in some of our poorest electoral wards, in which less than a third of those registered bother to vote. No globally competitive economy can survive when around 50% of school-leavers fail to achieve basic qualifications.

Overall, however, this book has been about the importance of the local, as the context in which 'God takes place'. Working for the good of the city begins and ends in the local – but a 'local' increasingly characterised by global currents: economic change, recession, cultural pluralism, mobility and migration. People of faith have a choice whether or not to allow themselves to be carried along with these currents, although our argument has been that as far as the urban church is concerned it cannot help but have the concerns of the 'good city' at the heart of all that it does. This is faith that is not just about 'religion' in a narrow sense but about practising the virtues of justice, trust and commitment – or what the apostle Paul might call reaping the fruits of faith, hope and love. It begins with a faith in God, but puts its hope in the positive power of regeneration and renewal for a better future, and in the long-term 'dividend' from investing resources and pride in the well-being of their communities. Yet ultimately, it is simply a call to love one's neighbours as oneself, and of allowing oneself to be a channel through which the 'good city' – the new Jerusalem – takes place.

Bibliography

ACAGUPA (Archbishop of Canterbury's Advisory Group on Urban Priority Areas) (1990), *Living Faith in the City*, London: Church House Publishing.

ACUPA (Archbishop's Commission on Urban Priority Areas) (1985), *Faith in the City: A Call for Action by Church and Nation*, London: Church House Publishing.

Alibhai-Brown, Yasmin (2008), 'No-go areas are all in the bishop's mind', *Independent* 7 January.

Alinsky, Saul (1989), *Rules for Radicals*, London: Vintage (first published in 1971 by Random House).

Amos, Clare (2004), *The Book of Genesis*, London: Epworth.

Apuzzo, Jason Alexander (2001), 'Metropolis: The Foundation of the *Avant-garde*' *Neurosurgery* 49 (4), 992–5.

Atherton, John R. (2000), *Public Theology for Changing Times*, London: SPCK.

Atherton, John R. (2003), *Marginalization*, London: SCM Press.

Atherton, John R. (2009) 'Are we happier, Mr. Brown?' in Peter M. Scott, Elaine L. Graham and Christopher R. Baker (eds), *Remoralising Britain? Political, Ethical and Theological Perspectives on New Labour*, London and New York: Continuum, 83–96.

Audi, Robert (1997), 'Liberal Democracy and the Place of Religion in Politics' in Robert Audi and Nicholas Wolterstorff (eds), *Religion in the Public Square: Debating Church and State*, Lanham: Rowman and Littlefield, 1–66.

AUN (Anglican Urban Network) (2008) *Transforming Urban Mission*, London: Mission and Public Affairs, Church of England.

Baker, Christopher R. (2007), *The Hybrid Church in the City*, London: Ashgate.

Baker, Christopher R. and Graham, Elaine L. (2004), *Religious Capital in Regenerating Communities*, Manchester: William Temple Foundation/Northwest Development Agency.

Ballard, Paul H. and Husselbee, Lesley (2008), *Community and Ministry: An Introduction to Community Work in a Christian Context*, London: SPCK.

BBC *News* (2003), 'Liverpool named capital of culture' (online), 4 June, available at: http://news.bbc.co.uk/1/hi/entertainment/arts/2959944.stm [accessed 01/05/09].

BBC Liverpool (2009), 'Year of Culture. How was it for you?' (online), available at: http://www.bbc.co.uk/liverpool/content/articles/2008/12/23/culture_end_of_year_feature.shtml [accessed 24/01/09].

Bedford-Strohm, Heinrich (2007), 'Nurturing Reason: The Public Role of Religion in the Liberal State', *Ned Geref Teologiese Tydskrif* 48 (1 and 2), March–June, 25–41.

'Beentheredunit' (2007), 'Re: South Oxhey' (online), 24 February, available at: http://www.chavtowns.co.uk/modules.php?name=News&file=article&sid=395 [accessed 24/01/09].

Bentley, Timothy (1996), 'Green Urbanism and the Lessons of European Cities' in Richard T. Gates and Frederic Stout (eds), *The City Reader*, London: Routledge, 399–408.

Bergmann, Sigurd (2007), 'Theology in its Spatial Turn: Space, Place and Built Environments Challenging and Changing the Images of God', *Religion Compass* 1, 1–27.

Bergmann, Sigurd (2008), 'Making Oneself at Home in Environments of Urban Amnesia: Religion and Theology in City Space', *International Journal of Public Theology* 2 (1), 70–97.

Bianchini, F. and Parkinson, M. (1993), *Cultural Policy and Urban Regeneration: The West European Experience*, Manchester, Manchester University Press.

Billings, Alan (2009), *God and Community Cohesion: Help or Hindrance?* London: SPCK.

Bonhoeffer, Dietrich (1995), *Ethics*, London: SCM Press.

Breitenberg, E. Harold (2003), 'To Tell the Truth: Will the Real Public Theology Please Stand Up?' *Journal of the Society of Christian Ethics* 23 (2), 55–96.

Brett, Mark G. (2000), *Genesis: Procreation and the Politics of Identity*, London: Routledge.

Briggs, Sheila (2004), 'Taking the Train' in Kathryn Tanner (ed.), *Spirit in the Cities: Searching for Soul in the Urban Landscape*, Minneapolis: Augsberg Fortress Press, 1–19.

Carson, Rachel (1987 [1962]), *Silent Spring*, 25th Anniversary Edition, Houghton Mifflin.

Carter, Helen (2003), 'Gritty city wins the boho crown', *Guardian*, 26 May (online), available at: http://arts.guardian.co.uk/print/0,,4676828110427,00.html [accessed 26/05/03].

Casanova, José (1994), *Public Religions in the Modern World*, Chicago: University of Chicago Press.

Casanova, José (2006), 'Rethinking Secularization: A Global Comparative Perspective', *The Hedgehog Review*, Spring/Summer, 7–22.

Cavanaugh, William T. (1998), *Torture and Eucharist: Theology, Politics and the Body of Christ*, Oxford: Blackwell.

Cavanaugh, William T. (2003), 'Church' in Peter M. Scott and William T. Cavanaugh (eds), *The Blackwell Companion to Political Theology*, Oxford: Blackwell, 393–406.

Cavanaugh, William T. (2006), 'From One City to Two: Christian Reimagining of Political Space', *Political Theology* 7 (3), 299–321.

Centre for Cities (2009), *Cities Outlook 2009*, London: Centre for Cities.

Centre for Cultural Policy Research, University of Glasgow (2003), *The Cities Project: The Long-term Legacies of Glasgow 1990 European City of Culture* (online), available at: http://www.culturalpolicy.arts.gla.ac.uk/research/press_content_analysis_may03.pdf [accessed 27/11/06].

Chambers, Ed (2004), *Roots for Radicals*, New York: Continuum.

Chaplin, Jonathan (2008), 'Legal Monism and Religious Pluralism: Rowan Williams on Religion, Loyalty and Law', *International Journal of Public Theology* 2 (4), 418–41.

Chapman, Mark (2005), *Blair's Britain*, London: Darton, Longman and Todd.

Chapman, Mark (2008), *Doing God: Religion and Public Policy in Brown's Britain*, London: Darton, Longman and Todd.

Clark, David (2007), *Breaking the Mould of Regeneration: The Legacy, Role and Future of the Human City Institute*, Birmingham: HCI.

Clark, Helen (2007), Address at Opening Ceremony of the Third Asia-Pacific Regional Interfaith Dialogue, 29 May, available at http://www.scoop.co.nz/stories/print.html?path=PA0705/S00741.htm [accessed 14 June 2008].

Clark, Henry (1993), *The Church Under Thatcher*, London: SPCK.

Conservative Party Social Justice Working Group (2007), *Breakthrough Britain: Ending the Costs of Social Breakdown*, London: Centre for Social Justice.

Cooper, N. (1992), *All Mapped Out? A Critical Evaluation of the Methodist Mission Alongside the Poor Programme*, Manchester: William Temple Foundation.

Cox, Harvey (1965), *The Secular City*, London: SCM Press.

Cox, Stephen (2006), 'Review of Faithful Cities', *Fulcrums* (online), available at: http://www.fulcrum-anglican.org.uk/news/2006/20061015cox.cfm?doc=146 [accessed October 24th 2006].

Cresswell, Tim (1996), *In Place / Out of Place*, University of Minnesota Press.

CULF (Archbishops' Commission on Urban Life and Faith) (2006), *Faithful Cities: A Call for Celebration, Vision and Justice*, Peterborough: Methodist Publishing House.

Davey, Andrew (2000), *Urban Christianity and Global Order*, London: SPCK.

Davey, Andrew (2004), 'Editorial: On the Faultlines of the Global City', *Crucible*, July–September, 3–12.

Davey, Andrew (2007), '*Faithful Cities*: Locating Everyday Faithfulness', *Contact: Practical Theology and Pastoral Care* 152, 9–20.

Davey, Andrew (2008), 'Better Place: Performing the Urbanisms of Hope', *International Journal of Public Theology* 2 (1), 27–46.

Davies, John Gordon (1968), *The Secular Use of Church Buildings*, London: SCM Press.

Davies, John Gordon (1973), *Everyday God: Encountering the Holy in World and Worship*, London: SCM Press.

Davis, Francis, Paulhus, Elizabeth and Bradstock, Andrew (2008), *Moral But No Compass: Government, Church and the Future of Welfare*, Chelmsford: Matthew James.

Davis, Mike (2006), *Planet of Slums*, London: Verso.

de Bres, Joris (2007), 'Human Rights and Religious Diversity', *Aotearoa Ethnic Network Journal* 2 (2), 9–14.

de Gruchy, John (2007), 'Public Theology as Christian Witness: Exploring the Genre', *International Journal of Public Theology* 1 (1), 26–41.

Demos, 'Manchester is favourite with "new bohemians" ' (online), available at: http://www.demos.co.uk/media/pressreleases/bohobritain [accessed 26/05/03].

Department of Media, Culture and Sport, *Government and the Value of Culture* (2004), (online), available at: http://www.culture.gov.uk/NR/rdonlyres/DE2ECA497F3D-46BF-9D11-A3AD80BF54D6/0/valueofculture.pdf [accessed 10/09/06].

Dinham, Adam and Lowndes, Vivien (2009), 'Faith and the Public Realm' in Adam Dinham, Robert Furbey and Vivien Lowndes (eds), *Faith in the Public Realm: Controversies, Policies and Practices*, Bristol: Policy Press, 1–19.

EACCC (External Advisory Committee on Cities and Communities) (2006), *From Restless Communities to Resilient Places: Building a Stronger Future for all Canadians*, Ottowa: Infrastructure Canada.

Farnell, Richard, Furbey, Rob, Shams Al-Haqq Hills, Stephen, Macey, Marie and Smith, Greg (2003), *'Faith' in Urban Regeneration? Engaging Faith Communities in Urban Regeneration*, Bristol: The Policy Press.

Field, John (2003), *Social Capital*, London: Routledge.

Florida, Richard (2002), *The Rise of the Creative Class: And How it's Transforming Work, Leisure, Community and Everyday Life*, New York: Basic Books.

Forrester, Duncan (2001), *On Human Worth: A Christian Vindication of Equality*, London: SCM Press.

Forrester, Duncan (2004), 'The Scope of Public Theology', *Studies in Christian Ethics* 17 (2), 5–19.

Freire, Paulo (1996 [1972]), *Pedagogy of the Oppressed*, New York: Continuum.

Furbey, Robert (1999), 'Urban "Regeneration": Reflections on a Metaphor', *Critical Social Policy* 19 (4), 419–45.

Furbey, Robert and Macey, Marie (2005), 'Religion and Urban Regeneration: A Place for Faith?' *Policy and Politics* 33 (1), 95–116.

Furbey Robert et al. (2006), *Faith as Social Capital: Connecting or Dividing?* Joseph Rowntree Foundation, Bristol: The Policy Press.

Furbey, Robert (2009), 'Controversies of "Public Faith" ' in Dinham, Furbey and Lowndes (2009), 21–40.

Gamaliel Foundation (2008), 'The Gamaliel Philosophy' (online), available at: http://www.gamaliel.org/Foundation/philosophy.htm [accessed 09/11/08].

Garner, Rod (2004), *Facing the City: Urban Mission in the Twenty-first Century*, London: Epworth.

Garner, Steve, Cowles, James, Lung, Barbara and Stott, Marina (2009), *Sources of Resentment and Perceptions of Ethnic Minorities among Poor White People in England*, London: Department for Communities and Local Government.

Garnett, J., Grimley, M., Harris, A., Whyte, W. and Williams, S. (eds), (2006), *Redefining Christian Britain: Post 1945 Perspectives*, London: SCM Press.

Gay, Doug (2007), 'Faith in, with and under Gordon Brown: A Scottish Presbyterian/ Calvinist Reflection', *International Journal of Public Theology* 1 (3–4), 306–20.

Giles, Richard (1996), *Re-Pitching the Tent: Reordering the Church Building for Worship and Mission in the New Millennium*, Norwich: Canterbury Press.

Gillett, Richard W. (2005), *The New Globalization: Reclaiming the Lost Ground of our Christian Social Tradition*, Cleveland, OH: Pilgrim Press.

Glasson, Barbara and Bradbury, John (2007), 'Liverpool: The Lived Experience of Culture' in Core Cities Theology Network (ed.), *Cities of Culture: Whose Vision, Which Agenda?* Newcastle, 27–36.

Gorringe, Tim (2004), *A Theology of Culture*, London: Ashgate.

Gorringe, Tim (2008), 'Salvation by Bricks: Theological Reflections on the Planning Process', *International Journal of Public Theology* 2 (1), 98–118.

Graham, Elaine (1996), 'Theology in the City: Ten Years after *Faith in the City*', *Bulletin of the John Rylands Research Institute* 78 (1), 179–97.

Graham, Elaine (2002), *Representations of the Post/Human: Monsters, Aliens and Others in Popular Culture*, Manchester: Manchester University Press.

Graham, Elaine (2004), 'Public Theology in an Age of "Voter Apathy" ' in W. Storrar and A. Morton (eds), *Public Theology in the 21st Century*, Edinburgh: T & T Clark, 385–403.

Graham, Elaine (2007), 'Power, Knowledge and Authority in Public Theology', *International Journal of Public Theology* 1 (1), 42–62.

Graham, Elaine (2008a), 'What Makes a Good City? Reflections on Urban Life and Faith', *International Journal of Public Theology* 2 (1), 7–26.

Graham, Elaine (2008b), 'Rethinking the Common Good: Theology and the Future of Welfare', *Colloquium* 40 (2), 133–56.

Graham, Elaine (2009a), 'Doing God? Public Theology under Blair' in Peter M. Scott, Elaine L. Graham and Christopher R. Baker (eds), *Remoralising Britain? Political, Ethical and Theological Perspectives on New Labour*, London and New York: Continuum, 1–18.

Graham, Elaine L. (2009b), 'Health, Wealth or Wisdom? Religion and the Paradox of Prosperity', *International Journal of Public Theology* 3 (1), 5–23.

Graham, Elaine (2009c), 'A Window on the Soul: Four Politicians on Religion and Public Life', *International Journal of Public Theology* 3 (2), forthcoming.

Graham, Elaine and Lowe, Stephen (2004), *What Makes a Good City? The Chicago Experience*, Manchester: Manchester Centre for Public Theology.

Graham, Elaine, Walton, Heather and Ward, Frances (2005), *Theological Reflection: Methods*, London: SCM Press.

Graham, Elaine, Walton, Heather and Ward, Frances (2007), *Theological Reflection: Sources*, London: SCM Press.

Guardian (2003), 'Liverpool named European capital of culture', 4 June.

Hanley, Lynsey (2007), *Estates: An Intimate History*, London: Granta.

Harris, Harriet (2006), 'Ambivalence over Virtue' in J. Garnett, M. Grimley, A. Harris, W. Whyte and S. Williams (eds), *Redefining Christian Britain: Post 1945 Perspectives*, London: SCM Press, 210–21.

Harvey, Anthony (1989), *Theology in the City*, London: SPCK.

Harvey, David (2008), 'The Right to the City', *New Left Review* 53, 23–40.

Hasler, Joe (2006), *Crying out for a Polycentric Church: Christ Centred and Cultural Focused*, Church in Society.

Hauerwas, Stanley (1981), *Vision and Virtue: Essays in Christian Theological Reflection*, Notre Dame, IN: University of Notre Dame Press.

Hauerwas, Stanley (1984), *The Peaceable Kingdom: A Primer in Christian Ethics*, London: SCM Press.

Hauerwas, Stanley (1991), *After Christendom? How the Church is to Behave if Freedom, Justice and a Christian Nation are Bad Ideas*, Nashville: Abingdon Press.

Hauerwas, Stanley and Wells, Sam (eds) (2004), *The Blackwell Companion to Christian Ethics*, Oxford: Blackwell.

Hefner, Philip (2003), *Technology and Human Becoming*, Minneapolis: Fortress Press.

Heyer, Kristin E. (2004), 'How does Theology Go Public? Rethinking the Debate between David Tracy and George Lindbeck', *Political Theology* 5 (3), 307–27.

Higton, Mike (2008), 'Rowan Williams and Sharia: Defending the Secular', *International Journal of Public Theology* 2 (4), 400–17.

Inge, John (2003), *A Christian Theology of Place*, London: Ashgate.

Institute for Fiscal Studies (2008), *Poverty and Inequality in the UK*, London: Institute for Fiscal Studies.

James, O. (2007), *Affluenza: How to be Successful and Stay Sane*, London: Vermilion.

Katwala, Sunder (2006), 'Faith in Democracy: The Legitimate Role of Religion', *Public Policy Research*, December–February, 246–51.

Klein, Joe (2008), 'Passing the Torch', *Time* magazine, 17 November, 24–5.

Lally, Pat (1991), 'Glasgow's Glasgow', *New York Review of Books*, 26 September (online), available at: http://www.nybooks.com/articles/3165 [accessed 27/11/06].

Lammy, David (2007), *Faith and Politics: The Tawney Lecture 2007*, London: Christian Socialist Movement.

Layard, R. (2005), *Happiness: Lessons from a New Science*, London: Allen Lane.

Layard, Richard and Dunn, Judy (2009), *A Good Childhood: Searching for Values in a Competitive Age*, Harmondsworth: Penguin.

Ledwith, Margaret (2005) *Community Development*, Bristol: BASW/Policy Press.

Leech, Kenneth (2006), 'The Soul and the City: Urban Ministry and Theology 1956–2006', Samuel Ferguson Lecture 2006, University of Manchester (19 October 2006).

Lewis, Christopher (2004), 'Christianity as Heritage', *Theology*, vol. CVII, no. 835, 30–6.

Lindbeck, George (1984), *The Nature of Doctrine: Religion and Theology in a Post-Liberal Age*, Philadelphia: Westminster Press.

Lindbeck, George (1989), 'The Church's Mission to a Postmodern Culture' in Frederich Burnham, (ed.), *Postmodern Theology: Christian Faith in a Pluralist World*, San Francisco: Harper and Row, 37–55.

Livezey, Lowell W. (2000), 'The New Context of Urban Religion' in L. W. Livezey (ed.), *Public Religion and Urban Transformation: Faith in the City*, New York: New York University Press, 3–25.

Lock, Liz and Henner, Mishka (2006), *One Hundred Years: One Hundred Faces* Manchester: Common Eye Books.

Lowe, Stephen (2009), '*Moral But No Compass*: A Report to the Church of England from the Von Hügel Institute', London: Church House, GS Misc. 912.

Lowe, Stephen (2002), 'Is the Church Vital to the Process of Urban Regeneration?' *Modern Believing* 43 (4), 24–32.

Lowles, Nick (2008), 'Where Now?' *Searchlight*, June (online), available at: http://www.searchlightmagazine.com/index.php?link=template&story=233 [accessed 01/05/09].

Manchester City Council (2006), *Manchester's Cultural Strategy: Introduction* (online), available at: http://www.manchester.gov.uk/regen/culture/strategy [accessed 07/09/06].

Marty, Martin E. (1974), 'Reinhold Niebuhr: Public Theology and the American Experience', *The Journal of Religion* 54 (4), 332–59.

Massey, Doreen (2001), 'Living in Wythenshawe' in I. Borden, J. Kerr, J. Rendell and A. Piraro (eds), *The Unknown City: Contesting Architecture and Social Space*, Cambridge: MIT Press, ch. 28.

Mathewes, Charles T. (2008), *A Theology of Public Life*, Cambridge: Cambridge University Press.

Mawson, Andrew (2008), *The Social Entrepreneur: Making Communities Work*, London: Atlantic Books.

McCurry, Ruth (2007), 'Faithful Cities: Child of Faith in the City', *Contact: Practical Theology and Pastoral Care* 152, 40–9.

McIntosh, Esther (2008), 'Philosophers, Politicians and Archbishops: Religious Reasons in the Public Sphere', *International Journal of Public Theology* 2 (4), 465–83.

Meadows, Donella (ed.) (2005 [1972]), *Limits to Growth: The 30 Year Update*, London: Earthscan.

Mellor, Rosemary (2002), 'Hypocritical City: Cycles of Urban Exclusion' in J. Peck and K. Ward (eds), *City of Revolution: Restructuring Manchester*, Manchester: Manchester University Press, 214–35.

Mendieta, Eduardo (2001), 'Invisible Cities: A Phenomenology of Globalization from Below', *City* 5 (1), 7–26.

Methodist Church (1997), *The Cities*, London: NCH Action for Children.

Michaelson, J., Abdallah, S., Steuer, N., Thompson, S. and Marks, N. (2009), *National Accounts of Well-being: Bringing Real Wealth onto the Balance Sheet*, London: New Economics Foundation.

Milbank, John (1990), *Theology and Social Theory*, Oxford: Blackwell.

Milbank, John, Ward, Graham and Pickstock, Catherine (1999), *Radical Orthodoxy: A New Theology*, London: Routledge.

Miles, Steven and Paddison, Ronan (2005), 'The Rise and Rise of Culture-led Urban Regeneration', *Urban Studies* 42 (5–6), 83–39.

Mooney, Gerry (2004), 'Cultural Policy as Urban Transformation? Critical Reflections on Glasgow, European City of Culture 1990', *Local Economy* 19 (4), 327–40.

Morisy, Ann (2004), *Journeying Out: A New Approach to Christian Mission*, London: Continuum.

Nachowitz, Todd (2007), 'New Zealand as a Multireligious Society: Recent Census Figures and Some Relevant Implications', *Aotearoa Ethnic Network Journal* 2 (2).

Nazir-Ali, Michael (2008), 'Extremism flourished as UK lost Christianity', *Sunday Telegraph*, 6 January (online), available at: http://www.telegraph.co.uk/news/uknews/1574695/Extremism-flourished-as-UK-lost-Christianity.html [accessed 24/01/09].

Niebuhr, H. Richard (1951), *Christ and Culture*, San Francisco: Harper & Row.

Niebuhr, Reinhold (1932), *Moral Man and Immoral Society: A Study in Ethics and Politics*, London: Scribner.

Northcott, Michael (ed.), (1997) *Urban Theology: A Reader*, London: Cassell.

NZDAP (New Zealand Diversity Action Programme) (2007), *Religious Diversity in New Zealand: Statement on Religious Diversity*, available at: http://www.hrc.co.nz/hrc_new/hrc/cms/files/documents/25-May-2007_08-24-50_NSRD_booklet.pdf [accessed 21/06/08].

Obama, Barack (1990), 'Why Organize? Problems and Promise in the Inner City' in Peg Knoepfle (ed.), *After Alinsky: Community Organizing in Illinois*, Washington: Institute for Public Affairs, 35–40.

Peck, Jamie and Ward, Kevin (eds) (2002), *City of Revolution: Restructuring Manchester*, Manchester: Manchester University Press.

Peck, M. Scott (1994), *A World Waiting to be Born: The Search for Civility*, London: Arrow Books.

Putnam, R. (2000), *Bowling Alone*, New York: Simon and Schuster.

Reader, John (1997), *Beyond all Reason: The Limits of Post-Modern Theology*, Cardiff: Aureus.

Richards, Alex (2006), 'Culture as Circus' (online), available at: http://www.spunk.org/texts/pubs/hn/sp000025.txt [accessed 10/09/06].

Rogers, Richard (1997), *Cities for a Small Planet*, London: Faber.

Russell, Hilary (1995), *Poverty Close to Home*, London: Continuum.

Sacks, Jonathan (2003), *The Dignity of Difference: How to Avoid the Clash of Civilizations*, London: Continuum.

Sadgrove, Michael (2006) in Stephen Platten and Christopher Lewis (eds), *Dreaming Spires? Cathedrals in a New Age*, London: SPCK.

Sandercock, Leonie (2003), *Cosmopolis II: Mongrel Cities in the 21st Century*, London: Continuum.

Sandercock, Leonie (2006), 'Spirituality and the Urban Professions: The Paradox at the Heart of Planning', *Planning Theory & Practice* 7 (1), 65–7.

Sanks, T. H. (1993), 'David Tracy's Theological Project: An Overview and Some Implications', *Theological Studies* 54, 698–727.

Sassen, Saskia (2006), *Cities in a World Economy*, London: Sage, 3rd edn.

Schopen, Fay (2009), 'City of culture prize aims to bring regeneration to the regions', *The Times* (online), 23 January, available at: http://business.timesonline.co.uk/tol/business/industry_sectors/leisure/article5569465.ece [accessed 24/01/09].

Schreiter, Robert J. (1985), *Constructing Local Theologies*, New York: Orbis Books.

Scott, Peter Manley (2008), 'The City's Grace? Recycling the Urban Ecology', *International Journal of Public Theology* 2 (1), 119–35.

Sedgwick, Peter (1998), 'Theology and Society' in David F. Ford (ed.), *The Modern Theologians*, vol. 2, Oxford: Blackwell, 286–305.

Selby, Peter (1996), *Rescue: Jesus and Salvation Today*, London: SPCK.

Sentamu, John (2009), 'Regaining a Big Vision for Britain', Smith Institute Lecture, 13 January (online), available at: http://www.archbishopofyork.org/2127 [accessed 19/01/09].

Sheldrake, Philip (2000), *Spaces for the Sacred: Place, Memory, Identity*, London: SCM Press.

Sheldrake, Philip (2005), 'Space and the Sacred: Cathedrals and Cities', *Contact: Practical Theology and Pastoral Care* 147, 8–17.

Shortt, Rupert (2008), *Rowan's Rule: The Biography of the Archbishop*, London: Hodder & Stoughton.

Smith, Greg (2004), 'Faith in Community and Communities of Faith? Government Rhetoric and Religious Identity in Urban Britain', *Journal of Contemporary Religion* 19 (2), 185–204.

Smith, James K. A. (2004), *Introducing Radical Orthodoxy: Mapping a Post-Secular Theology*, Grand Rapids, MI: Baker Academic.

Soja, Edward (2003), 'Writing the City Spatially', *City* 7 (3), 269–81.

Steele, Jess (2009), 'Social Justice, Social Control or the Pursuit of Happiness? The Goals and Values of the Regeneration Industry' in Peter M. Scott, Elaine L. Graham and Christopher R. Baker (eds), *Remoralising Britain? Political, Ethical and Theological Perspectives on New Labour*, London and New York: Continuum, 97–119.

'supacreep' (2005), 'Re: South Oxhey' (online) 10 December, available at http://www.chavtowns.co.uk/modules.php?name=News&file=article&sid=395 [accessed 24/01/09].

Tanner, Kathryn (ed.) (2004), *Spirit in the Cities: Searching for Soul in the Urban Landscape*, Minneapolis: Fortress Press.

Taylor, Michael (1996), *Not Angels but Agencies*, London: SPCK.

Teasdale, Jason (2006), 'Former Culture Director Warns Liverpool Not to Forget its Roots', *The Enquirer*, 7–13 September, 4.

Toulmin, Stephen (1990), *Cosmopolis: The Hidden Agenda of Modernity*, Chicago: University of Chicago Press.

Toynbee, Polly (2005), 'In the Name of God', *Guardian*, 22 July.

Toynbee, Polly and Walker, David (2008), *Unjust Rewards: Exposing Greed and Inequality in Britain Today*, London: Granta.

Tunstall, Rebecca and Coulter, Alice (2006), *Twenty-five Years on Twenty Estates*, Bristol: The Policy Press.

Tyndale, Wendy (ed.) (2006), *Visions of Development: Faith-based Development*, London: Ashgate.

UN-HABITAT (2008), *The State of the World's Cities 2008/09: Harmonious Cities*, London: Earthscan.

Urban Bishops' Panel (2002), *The Urban Renaissance and the Church of England: A Discussion Paper*, GS Misc. 1446, London: General Synod of the Church of England.

van Wolde, Ellen (1996), *Stories of the Beginning: Genesis 1—11 and Other Creation Stories*, trans. John Bowden, London: SCM Press.

Vincent, John (ed.) (2003), *Faithfulness in the City*, Hawarden: Monad Press.

Walker, Andrew (ed.) (2005), *Spirituality in the City*, London: SPCK.

Ward, Graham (2000), *Cities of God*, London: Routledge.

Warner, R. Stephen (2000), 'Building Religious Communities at the Turn of the Century' in L. W. Livezey (ed.), *Public Religion and Urban Transformation*, New York: New York University Press, 295–307.

Westwood, Andy and Nathan, Max (2002), *Manchester: Ideopolis? Developing a Knowledge Capital*, London: The Work Foundation.

Wheeler, Stephen (1996), 'Planning Sustainable and Livable Cities' in Richard T. Gates and Frederic Stout (eds), *The City Reader*, London: Routledge, 486–96.

Wickham, E. R. (1958), *Church and People in an Industrial City*, London: Hodder & Stoughton.

Wilks-Heeg, Stuart and North, Peter (2004), 'Cultural Policy and Urban Regeneration', *Local Economy* 19 (4), 305–11.

Williams, Prue (2004), *Victoria Baths: Manchester's Water Palace*, Reading: Spire Books.

Williams, Rowan (2006a), *Cities and Towns*, Lords debate, 19 May, *Hansard*, 19/05/06:53 (online), available at: http://www.publications.parliament.uk/pa/ld199900/ldhansrd/pdvn/lds06/text/6051901.htm [accessed 20/05/06].

Williams, Rowan (2006b), 'Secularism, Faith and Freedom', Pontifical Academy of Social Sciences, Rome, 23 November (online), available at:
http://www.archbishopofcanterbury.org/654 [accessed 01/05/09].

Wintour, Patrick (2009), 'In Liverpool's footsteps: now every city can aim to be Britain's capital of culture', *Guardian*, 7 January, 11.

Wolterstorff, Nicholas (1997), 'The Role of Religion in Decision and Discussion of Political Issues' in Robert Audi and Nicholas Wolterstorff (eds), *Religion in the Public Square: Debating Church and State*, Lanham: Rowman and Littlefield, 67–120.

World Commission on Environment and Development (1987), *Our Common Future*, Oxford: Oxford University Press.

Young, Audrey (2006), 'Clark calls for action to combat extremism', *New Zealand Herald*, 27 December.

Notes

1   Frequently attributed to Temple although most sources are unable to identify its origins. See also p. 8.

2   Some visits were made by members of CULF to local projects, special consultative seminars were held and contributions were invited from churches, community groups and individuals. Some of this evidence formed the basis of the text boxes that punctuate the report.

3   Much of this research suggests that those who belong to religious groups or profess a religious faith are more likely to report higher levels of happiness and well-being. See Atherton, 2009 and Graham, 2009b.

4   See later, Chapter 8.

5   On religion and secularism, see also Furbey, 2009 and McIntosh, 2008.

6   During the Report's preparation, Clark stated that government did need to address the question of religious extremism to prevent the kind of second- and third-generation Muslim activism seen in the UK (Young, 2006).

7   http://www.manchester.gov.uk/health/jhu/intelligence/city.htm [accessed 25/11/06].

8   http://www.liverpool08.com/.

9   See also www.victoriabaths.org.uk.

10   www.thechurchstmarys.co.uk.

11   As, for example, the Black majority churches' involvement in organisations such as Operation Black Vote, REACH (Raising the Aspirations of Black Boys and Young Black Men) and Faithworks.

12   See, for example, the Institute for Urban Ministry in Pretoria, South Africa: http://www.tlf.org.za/ium.htm; the Global Network for Public Theology; Tyndale, 2006.

13   http://www.stmartinscentre.org.uk/index.php?option=com_content&task=vie&id=16&Itemid=28.

Index of Names

Index of Subjects